Reimagining Popular Notions of American Intellectualism

Reimagining Popular Notions of AMERICAN INTELLECTUALISM: literacy, education, and class

Kelly Susan Bradbury

SOUTHERN ILLINOIS UNIVERSITY PRESS *CARBONDALE*

Southern Illinois University Press
www.siupress.com

Portions of chapter 4 were previously published as "Intellectualizing Adult Basic Literacy Education: A Case Study," *Community Literacy Journal* 6.2 (Spring 2012): 1–21.
Portions of chapter 6 were previously published as "Outsmarting Pop Culture's 'Be Stupid' Pedagogy," *Academic Exchange Quarterly* 15.3 (Fall 2011): 69–74.

Printed in the United States of America

19 18 17 16 4 3 2 1

Cover design by Johanna Tesfaye

Library of Congress Cataloging-in-Publication Data
Names: Bradbury, Kelly, author.
Title: Reimagining popular notions of American intellectualism : literacy, education, and class / Kelly Susan Bradbury.
Description: Carbondale, Illinois : Southern Illinois University Press, 2016. | Includes bibliographical references and index.
Identifiers: LCCN 2015033672| ISBN 9780809334889 (paperback) | ISBN 9780809334896 (e-book)
Subjects: LCSH: Learning and scholarship—United States—History. | Learning and scholarship—Social aspects—United States. | Adult education—United States—History. | Literacy—United States—History. | Education—Social aspects—United States. | United States—Intellectual life. | BISAC: LANGUAGE ARTS & DISCIPLINES / Literacy. | LANGUAGE ARTS & DISCIPLINES / Study & Teaching.
Classification: LCC AZ505 .B73 2016 | DDC 001.2—dc23
LC record available at http://lccn.loc.gov/2015033672

For Jack and Evelyn,
who have helped me to reimagine work, life, and love

Contents

Acknowledgments

THE INSPIRATION FOR THIS BOOK has always been my students. I have been lucky enough to work with many over the years, and to work with them in both college and community classrooms. It is their brilliance, their passion, and their stories that have motivated and guided me in my work. I am thankful for them and for all they have taught me. I am grateful, in particular, for the students who have allowed me to share their thoughts and their stories in this book, including those at the Lindberg Center and those at the College of Staten Island, especially Dhiwya, Gina, Kawsar, Joseph, and Lucinda.

Writing this book has been among the hardest and most humbling of my accomplishments, and it would not have been possible were it not for my mentors and peers. Michael Keller deserves special thanks for being my first intellectual mentor and for encouraging me to pursue a thesis project on anti-intellectualism that greatly informed this work. I owe much, also, to Kay Halasek and Beverly Moss, who offered meaningful feedback, support, and encouragement, and who continue to serve as personal as well as professional mentors. I am most indebted to Harvey J. Graff for introducing me to literacy studies, believing in this project from the start, and patiently guiding me through its development. As my advisor and mentor, he gave generously of his time and challenged me as a scholar, and for that I am eternally grateful. I cannot thank enough my Ohio State cohort, who not only supported me in the writing of this project, but who also have helped me grow personally and professionally. For their time, support, generosity, and friendship, I thank in particular Sheila Bock Alarid, Katie Comer, Michael Harker, Wendy Wolters Hinshaw, and Kate White.

My work on this project has been supported, in part, by several research grants. For giving me time and money to research and write, I thank Ohio State's Graduate School and Center for the Study and Teaching of Writing, the American Association of University Women, and the Professional Staff Congress of the City University of New York (CUNY). For his editorial guidance and support I thank Karl Kageff of Southern Illinois University Press. I am indebted, also, to the reviewers who read my work carefully and generously and provided feedback that helped shape and strengthen the project.

I give thanks, too, to my family. Together, my parents and siblings are my foundation. They have loved me unconditionally, supported me generously, and demonstrated genuine faith in me. They have always been my biggest—and loudest—cheerleaders.

And finally, I give thanks for the loves of my life. Scot and I met as graduate students pursuing our individual intellectual interests; since then, we have partnered on a new journey, one for which we challenge and support each other in the most meaningful ways. Our children, Jack and Evelyn, have opened our hearts and our minds and truly inspired us to reimagine our lives. We wish for them a life full of exploration and opportunity.

Reimagining Popular Notions of American Intellectualism

INTRODUCTION

WHEN I ASKED MY HONORS composition students at the College of Staten Island to draw visual representations of *intellectualism* and *anti-intellectualism* as they perceived the terms, their in-class drawings revealed several assumptions: Anti-intellectuals are preoccupied with vanity and consumerism or are lazy, media-obsessed couch potatoes. Intellectuals wear glasses, look like middle-aged professors, and are studious book readers and critical thinkers. The student drawings on the next page represent these trends well.

Not surprisingly, their depictions closely resemble popular media portrayals of intellectualism and anti-intellectualism (for example, on television shows like *Big Bang Theory*, *Community*, *How I Met Your Mother*, *The Simpsons*, and *Survivor*). Their drawings also resonate with popular critiques of American culture, and American education in particular: Americans are anti-intellectual and ignorant because of their consumerist attitudes toward education, because they don't read books (in traditional print), and because of their interactions with popular, social, and digital media. Couple these portrayals with the rhetoric of anti-intellectualism these students encounter locally: Staten Islanders are stereotyped as working-class, ill-spoken,

Student drawing of "intellectual."

Student drawing of "anti-intellectual."

uneducated "guidos"; additionally, the College of Staten Island (CSI) has been labeled by some the "College of Stupid Idiots." Consider too the message students receive from the recent general education curriculum "reform" implemented at CSI by the City University of New York (CUNY) administration. Despite protest by a majority of the faculty and some students across CUNY campuses, this reform reduced and, many argue, diluted the general education curriculum in an effort to increase graduation rates and ease student institutional transfer. It has been called by many an example of national trends toward "austerity education"—making public higher education more cost-effective with less concern for students' intellectual development.

Combined, the messages being sold to and bought by my students position them as anti-intellectual consumers of mind-numbing media and watered-down, career-focused degrees; they *do not* position them as consumers of meaningful, intellectual fare. It should come as no surprise, then, when students do not see themselves as members of—or participants in—an intellectual community, as indicated by written comments such as the following: "College has become a place where the anti-intellectual thrives, where it is all about receiving the college degree everyone needs for a job, and not about intellectual growth"; "In this fast-paced world, we rarely have the luxury of fostering intellectual pursuits. And if we do, it is usually more of a bonus and not the main goal"; and "[The author] was right in comparing the college environment to that of a consumer culture, where we, the students, are more focused on getting our money's worth, than on the exploration of new studies and ideas." In other words, these students (students in a prestigious honors program) do not view college as a place to exercise their intellect or pursue intellectual interests. Rather, they see it as a necessary step toward economic comfort.

A few years earlier, I asked some of the adult learners participating in community-run GED-preparation writing workshops what the word *intellectual* means. Their responses included the following: "I don't know. What does it mean?"; "No, I don't know what that is. Is it intellecture?"; "Okay, now, I know intelligent, but what's intellectual? You have to tell me. I'm not familiar with that term"; and "I know what intelligent means but we never talked about intellectual in high school so I wouldn't know the definition." Two students offered a definition. Wendell,[1] a sixty-year-old man who dropped out of school in seventh grade, described an intellectual as "a bookworm" with a high vocabulary. Carl, a young male in his twenties, distinguished a smart person from an intellectual:

> An intellectual attains his confidence through academics, so he's real aggressive toward his academics, but I think a smart person, he balances them out as far as his intelligence and his common sense. An intellectual person, they just grasp like education to be their way to freedom. An intellectual person is an aggressive learner, but with a smaller picture.

When I asked him if he considers himself an intellectual, Carl said,

> No, no, no, not at all. Because just for the simple fact that an intellectual person is just a person that sees school from one perspective, and you gotta look at it from multiple perspectives, multiple angles. An intellectual has fewer perspectives.

The fact that the GED adult learners I asked to define *intellectual* are unfamiliar with the term or define it in a way that excludes themselves is not surprising. They are part of a national public repeatedly labeled anti-intellectual and ignorant, and they have never been part of a community considered intellectual—including the GED community. Consequently, the knowledge they possess and the literacy and learning practices they engage in are devalued by much of society—and in some cases, by themselves.

Among the problems these examples illustrate is how popular notions of intellectualism affect the attitudes and actions of students, young and old, as they develop as thinkers. They also demonstrate what these beliefs do to our public understanding of learning, intelligence, and education. Equated with academics and academic success, with studying highbrow ideas at elite institutions of higher education, or with living a "life of the mind," contemporary views of intellectualism not only privilege the knowledge, learning sites, and educational experiences of the cultural elite, but they also devalue the educational experiences and spaces of the nonelite, including the students at CSI and those in the GED program. Of great importance to rhetoric, composition, and literacy studies scholars, these views also mediate the public's—and our students'—attitudes toward literacy; promote a powerful variant of the literacy myth that equates some literacy practices with intellectualism and others with non- or anti-intellectualism; and perpetuate problematic educational hierarchies that categorize some of our students, some of our research and teaching practices, and at times even our discipline as intellectually inferior.

Concerned by the consequences of popular, exclusionary notions of intellectualism, *Reimagining Popular Notions of American Intellectualism* calls us to mindfully reconsider and rethink what it means to be intellectual or to practice intellectualism in the twenty-first century. It proposes a more inclusive and egalitarian definition of intellectualism, deeming it an interest in, appreciation for, and engagement with learning, knowledge, deliberation, critical thinking, and inquiry. This definition better reflects the stated aspirations of educational institutions in this country and decidedly does not turn a blind eye to issues of class, elitism, and privilege. Our era demands a richer definition of intellectualism because so many forms of engaging with ideas and using our minds fall outside the rubrics of intellectualism many of us (including our students) follow. The definition proposed here will help us to challenge those rubrics and, instead, recognize and celebrate a broad range of intellectual activities and education institutions that represent well adult public education in the United States over time and place.

While some may argue that reimagining intellectualism is futile or unproductive, this book seeks to demonstrate the need for—and power of—changing the rhetoric that shapes Americans' understanding of and engagement with literacy and learning. To that end, the book surveys the evolution of contemporary limited notions of intellectualism and then reexamines the literacy and learning practices of three nonelite sites of adult public education through the lens of a more expansive definition of intellectualism. Taken together, these case studies challenge widespread beliefs that a majority of Americans are (and have been) ignorant and anti-intellectual and that the United States is void of intellectuals and intellectualism outside its elite universities. The book concludes with a call for the field to consider how we may aid students in recognizing, resisting, and reimagining for themselves what it means to be intellectual in the twenty-first century.

Reimagining Popular Notions of American Intellectualism, to be clear, is not a comprehensive treatment of intellectualism in American culture, past and present. Rather, its goal is to provide some historical context for the narrow vision of intellectualism exuded by students and the larger American public and then invite us to view intellectualism through a more expansive and helpful lens. Inspired by my work with students over the past fifteen years, this book, more specifically, is designed to encourage educators to reconsider the causes and consequences of popular notions of intellectualism in the United States, particularly in relation to their research and their work with students.

LANGUAGE, LITERACY, AND POWER

While rhetoric, composition, and literacy studies scholars have worked to contest characterizations of remedial writers as cognitively deficient and to draw attention to rhetoric that promotes and perpetuates inequalities, the field has not yet directly responded to the pervasive notions of intellectualism that greatly influence Americans'—and especially our students'—attitudes toward literacy and learning. Despite what some see as the field's marginalization within academia and within English departments, as members of the cultural elite who help to define intellectualism, we must participate in the public conversation and work to challenge the messages about literacy and learning perpetuated by this rhetoric.

This book builds on and extends the research of rhetoric, composition, and literacy studies scholars who have worked to expose and contest assumptions of cognitive abilities based on literacy and learning practices and who have publicized the social and cultural implications of such views (including, among others, Shaughnessy, Bartholomae, Petrosky, Mutnick). Mike Rose's scholarship, in particular, has for decades challenged definitions of intelligence that "drive broad cognitive wedges between those who do well in our schools and those who don't" ("Narrowing the Mind" 357). His broader research on the minds of American workers similarly opposes reductive notions of intelligence that influence our perceptions of others' cognitive abilities not only in school but also in the workplace and in our communities (*The Mind at Work* xix). Through these and other scholars, the field has worked to disentangle literacy and learning practices from assumptions about intelligence and cognitive abilities. The research in this book pushes the conversation further by challenging us to consider how our society makes similar assumptions about who can and does engage in intellectual work, and the consequences of those delineations.

This book also responds to the theories of those who have sought to challenge more broadly language and rhetoric practices that reinforce and perpetuate inequalities. Educational theorist Paulo Freire, in fact, argued that because the dominant class has the power to "define the world," it indeed defines intellectualism: "Only those who have power can decide what constitutes intellectualism. Once the intellectual parameters are set, those who want to be considered intellectuals must meet the requirements of the profile dictated by the elite class" (Freire and Macedo 122). Likewise, Antonio Gramsci argued that while all people have the potential to be intellectuals, the socially dominant class dictates who gets viewed as intellectual, protecting the power of the dominant class.

A primary force for challenging this rhetoric, these theorists contend, is to change it. As Freire argued, changing the "word" could help change the "world." And as Gramsci argued, the nondominant classes could become "new intellectuals" who would use rhetoric and communication to fight hegemony (10). Building on Gramsci's work, Victor Villanueva has contended rhetoric—often delivered through cultural institutions like schools, churches, and the media—is how "hegemonies are maintained" and consequently how they can be challenged. In his words, "Language used consciously, a matter of rhetoric, is a principal means—perhaps *the* means—by which change can begin to take place" (121).

In sum, this book reconsiders the field's conversations about language, literacy, and power in the twenty-first-century context in which narrow conceptions of intellectualism concretely influence Americans' views of and participation in literacy and learning practices. In response, it analyzes and works to disrupt rhetoric that privileges the experiences of those with the power to define intellectualism. It also pushes the field to consider related and previously unexamined questions including the following: In what ways have narrow, exclusionary views of intellectualism historically dictated how learning and literacy get defined, valued, and measured? How might a more meaningful and inclusive notion of intellectualism challenge or change this? What can rhetoric, composition, and literacy studies scholars learn from recognizing and responding to exclusionary views of intellectualism? What can students learn from recognizing, resisting, and redefining what it means to be an intellectual in the twenty-first century? It is my argument that reimagining intellectualism in the twenty-first century will help us—and our students—challenge the rhetoric that continues to mediate Americans' views of and participation in learning, literacy, and education.

INTRODUCTION TO CASE STUDIES

To engage the above questions, I studied three nontraditional, nonelite institutions of adult public education in the United States, past and present: the nineteenth-century lyceum, twentieth-century labor colleges, and twenty-first-century GED writing workshops. I chose the case-study approach because it helped me to illustrate and reflect more intensively on (1) ways Americans have, over time and place, perceived intellectualism, (2) the cultural beliefs, tensions, and assumptions that have informed those perceptions, and (3) the need for reimagining intellectualism in the twenty-first century. I chose as my sites nontraditional, nonelite institutions of adult public education because academics and cultural critics have by and large overlooked these types of institutions in their discussions about intellectualism primarily because they are associated with vocational and recreational learning (Grattan)—motivations for learning seen as opposed to intellectualism.

These three *particular* sites were selected for several reasons. First, they all have provided access to education to those whose education has been limited because of social, cultural, or material circumstances, such as lack of financial resources or access to affluent educational institutions. I also chose them because they represent well adult education in the United States across time and place. For example, the lyceum exemplifies the nineteenth-century widespread belief that self-improvement could be attained through acquiring "useful knowledge." It also epitomizes not only the popularity of lecturing and community gatherings as forms of learning at the time but also the desire of the period to open access to adult education to "all classes." The labor colleges' focus on educating workers, on utilizing progressive education philosophies like experiential and dialogic education, and the more formal structure of these schools typify prominent forms of adult education in the twentieth century. Finally, GED writing workshops are consistent with the more contemporary trend of pursuing education for job and life improvement.[2]

In order to reexamine the literacy and learning practices at these three sites, I conducted archival research for the historical chapters on lyceums and labor colleges and qualitative research for the contemporary chapter on GED writing workshops. The archival documents I accessed for my research on lyceums included lyceum meeting minutes, lecture transcripts, attendees' notes, reviews, and promotional materials. For the case study on twentieth-century labor colleges, my analysis centers on archival documents from Brookwood Labor College, the most popular and well-known American labor college. The documents accessed include course syllabi and materials, student writings, institution publications, promotional materials, reports, memos, and correspondence. The final case study draws from my work observing and interviewing students, teachers, and an administrator participating in a series of GED-preparation writing workshops at an adult education facility in a large midwestern town. Combined, these materials allowed me to examine each institution's educational mission (or purpose), its target audience, the knowledge it disseminated, and the literacy and learning practices it fostered.

Admittedly, this book is not the first to examine lyceums, labor colleges, or basic writing programs for their contributions to American education, literacy, or rhetoric; it is also not the first written by a rhetoric, composition, or literacy studies scholar. The American lyceum as a cultural institution has been treated extensively by Angela G. Ray. Karyn Hollis, Susan Kates, and Amy Wan have published important work on twentieth-century labor education. And highlighted earlier, several scholars have examined the pedagogy for, social and cultural consequences of, and assumptions about basic literacy education. *Reimagining Popular Notions of American Intellectualism* is, however, the first book to examine in depth—and in conjunction—these three important sites of adult public education, and to consider specifically their contributions to intellectualism in the United States. While these case studies do not (and cannot) represent the full range of literacy and learning activities in the United States over time and place, read collectively they can help us to better understand the history of popular notions of American intellectualism and also demonstrate the benefits of reconsidering and reimagining those notions.

CHAPTER OVERVIEW

Chapter 1, "Calls of Crisis and Decline in U.S. Literacy and Learning: Understanding Popular Notions of Intellectualism," surveys the longstanding beliefs, tensions, and assumptions in American cultural history that have helped shape the limited notions of intellectualism this book seeks to redefine. It also summarizes the consequences of these popular notions and makes note of the field's present contributions to relevant discussions.

Chapter 2, "Intellectualism and the Diffusion of Useful Knowledge: The Nineteenth-Century American Lyceum," is the first of the three case studies at the heart of the book. While scholars have credited the American lyceum with making knowledge accessible to the public, it has not been highlighted in discussions of American intellectualism because of its emphasis on disseminating useful knowledge and because of the prominence of entertainment on the lyceum stage in the last half of the century. An analysis of archival documents in this chapter reveals, however, that the lyceum's dissemination of useful knowledge encouraged and promoted a thirst for knowledge among participants and provided opportunities for active deliberation of the knowledge disseminated.

Drawing on archival documents from the most popular and widely recognized labor college in the United States, chapter 3, "Intellectualism and Education for a Practical Purpose: The Twentieth-Century Labor College," reenvisions the work of labor colleges as intellectual. These education institutions have been criticized for promoting doctrinaire thinking about issues relevant to the labor movement and for providing limited education for a practical purpose; consequently, they have not yet been recognized as sites of American intellectualism. This chapter demonstrates, however, how the curriculum and pedagogy of American labor colleges inspired workers to be active, analytical learners and motivated them to educate others through their activist work—cultivating intellectual inquiry and practice.

In chapter 4, "Intellectualism and Basic Literacy Education: Twenty-First-Century GED Writing Workshops," I dispute the assumption that a curriculum founded on basic literacy skills cannot be intellectual. Based on my interviews with and observations of participants in a series of GED-preparation writing workshops, I argue the content and curriculum used in these workshops encourages and supports various forms of intellectualism, including a desire to learn, personal investment in education, and critical thinking.

In chapter 5, "Making Connections: The Theory and Practice of Intellectualism in the United States," I highlight what analyzing the lyceum, labor colleges, and GED writing workshops in conjunction teaches us about literacy, learning, and intellectualism in the United States over time and place. Combined, I argue, these case studies complicate popular views of intellectualism and demonstrate the benefits of reimagining those views, particularly for the field of rhetoric, composition, and literacy studies.

Following my analysis of the contributions these case studies make toward reimagining intellectualism, the book concludes (in chapter 6, "Into the Classroom: Pedagogical Approaches to the Rhetoric of Intellectualism and Anti-intellectualism") with a reflection on my efforts to aid students in examining the rhetoric of anti-intellectualism and ignorance that surrounds them and its influence on their views and educational experiences. More specifically, I describe here two primary examples of assignments I have used in my college composition courses and offer my own and students' written reflections on what they learned from these assignments.

chapter one

CALLS OF CRISIS AND DECLINE IN U.S. LITERACY AND LEARNING

Understanding Popular Notions of Intellectualism

MY EXPERIENCES AS A LITERACY educator and researcher in recent years have led me not only to examine the consequences of limited notions of intellectualism but also to explore their roots. What, I have wondered, has led my students and much of the American public to assume they cannot—and will not—contribute to American intellectualism? Though it is inherently difficult to trace the history of an idea as it has circulated over time, the following survey of widespread calls of crisis and decline in U.S. literacy and learning helps elucidate for us the evolution of popular notions of intellectualism. The survey centers on three well-known texts that highlight the longstanding beliefs, tensions, and assumptions in our cultural history most responsible for how we think about ways of thinking and learning: *Anti-intellectualism in American Life*, *The Closing of the American Mind*, and *The Dumbest Generation*. These texts are particularly pertinent because of their notable and enduring popularity not only among academics and cultural critics but also among the American public.

ANTI-INTELLECTUALISM IN AMERICAN LIFE: RICHARD HOFSTADTER AND THE 1960s

Written as a "response to the political and intellectual conditions of the 1950's" (including the Inquisition, the post-Sputnik fear of a failing education system, and Eisenhower's defeat of the more "intellectual" Stevenson), historian Richard Hofstadter's 1963 Pulitzer Prize–winning *Anti-intellectualism in American Life* remains the foundational statement on anti-intellectualism in the United States. Even now, contemporary accusations of American anti-intellectualism and intellectual decline continue to draw from it. In it, Hofstadter maps the history of one of the longstanding tensions in our cultural history that has greatly influenced how we view intellectualism: a pervasive ambivalence toward intellectuals and intellectual life. It is this ambivalence, according to Hofstadter, that laid the foundation for a deep-seated anti-intellectualism in American culture.

The common attitudes and ideas that comprise anti-intellectualism, according to Hofstadter, are "a resentment and suspicion of the life of the mind and of those who are considered to represent it; and a disposition constantly to minimize the value of that life" (7). Inherent in the anti-intellectualism documented by Hofstadter are assumptions about intellectualism that have endured. An intellectual, as Hofstadter defined it, is someone who has "a sense of dedication to the life of the mind" and a desire to keep asking questions. He qualified this further, saying an intellectual lives *for* ideas, not *off* them, and lives for *ideas*, not *an idea*. Hofstadter also claimed practicality is not the basis of the intellectual's interest in ideas, even if the ideas have practical applications or consequences (27–31).

The equation of intellectualism with "the life of the mind" is central to Hofstadter's and many others' notions of intellectualism. Yet, this criterion significantly limits views of intellectualism. Associating intellectualism with a "life of the mind" implies that to be intellectual, a person must dedicate his or her life to the pursuit of ideas. Consequently, even though Hofstadter insisted intellectualism is not directly tied to a profession, he recognized that people often associate particular professions (and especially academics) with intellectualism because the work they do is considered "vitally dependent upon ideas" (26).

The cultural tendency to conflate intellectualism with academics and academic success is furthered by beliefs about what constitutes *intellect*. Distinguishing it from intelligence, Hofstadter said intellect is "the critical, creative, and contemplative side of mind." Intelligence, however, is an "excellence of mind that is employed within a fairly narrow, immediate, and predictable range; it is a manipulative, adjustive, unfailingly practical quality" (25). Hofstadter developed this distinction, stating:

> Whereas intelligence seeks to grasp, manipulate, re-order, adjust, intellect examines, ponders, wonders, theorizes, criticizes, imagines. Intelligence will seize the immediate meaning in a situation and evaluate it. Intellect evaluates evaluations, and looks for the meanings of situations as a whole. (25)

This distinction between intellect and intelligence, repeated in contemporary discussions of intellectualism, is not always so clear. What is clear is that intellect is believed to be *more than* intelligence. As a result, intellectualism gets conflated with academic excellence, power, and privilege (34). This, according to Hofstadter, has contributed to anti-intellectual sentiments concerning education: while our society has consistently charged schools with developing students' intelligence, whether or not they should "foster intellect" has been much debated (25).

Hofstadter's insistence that intellectuals do not pursue ideas for practical reasons has contributed to widespread beliefs that practical knowledge or knowledge pursued for a practical purpose cannot be intellectual. These beliefs continue to perpetuate hierarchies of knowledge and motivations for learning: practical knowledge and knowledge pursued for a practical purpose get labeled anti- or nonintellectual; abstract, "highbrow" knowledge and learning for its own sake are deemed intellectual.[1] These hierarchical delineations are a large part of the reason education institutions like American lyceums, labor colleges, and basic literacy programs have fallen outside the rubric of intellectualism.

Another issue highlighted by Hofstadter's history of anti-intellectualism in American culture is the propensity for a dichotomous view of matters of the mind. In this case Hofstadter promotes a view that pits anti-intellectualism against intellectualism and overlooks a larger spectrum of attitudes and ideas about learning. While he wrote that most people are not simply intellectual or anti-intellectual, but are more likely nonintellectual, or "infused with enough ambivalence about intellect and intellectuals to be swayed now this way and now that on current cultural issues" (19), he did not focus on nonintellectualism in his book and he did not address the nuances of intellectualism. Instead, he concentrated his book—his historical look at Americans' views of learning and the mind—on the more damning (and sensational) dichotomy: anti-intellectualism versus intellectualism.

Among the foundations Hofstadter laid with his history is the idea that anti-intellectualism has been part of American culture since its birth. While more contemporary critics tend to frame American anti-intellectualism and ignorance as the product of a descent from a previous intellectual golden age, Hofstadter argued it has *always* been rooted in American religion, business, politics, and education. According to him, this is because intellectualism is seen as hostile to much of what Americans value in those areas: the wisdom of the heart, experiential and practical knowledge, common sense, and an egalitarian educational system (19; 34). Hofstadter's history, then, has helped to popularize the notion that anti-intellectualism is deeply ingrained in the United States' cultural ethos. Contemporary critiques build off this notion, pointing out more contemporary manifestations of or contributors to American anti-intellectualism or ignorance. These accusations recycle the narrow definitions of intellectualism Hofstadter's book helped establish and that continue to influence Americans' engagement with literacy and learning.

THE CLOSING OF THE AMERICAN MIND: THE 1980s AND 1990s CULTURE WARS

While Richard Hofstadter's *Anti-intellectualism in American Life* has remained the foundational twentieth-century indictment of American attitudes toward intellectuals and intellectualism, Allan Bloom's *The Closing of the American Mind* has been the predominant twentieth-century critique of higher education's effects on American literacy and learning. Bloom's incisive salvo rose to the top of the best-seller list in 1987 following concerns about the state of American education, propagated, in part, by *Newsweek*'s 1975 sensational "Why Johnny Can't Write." Claiming "willy-nilly, the U.S. educational system is spawning a generation of semi-literates," the alarmist article alleged an urgent literacy crisis and called for a "back-to-basics" approach to language and literacy (Sheils). What followed was what came to be known as the "Culture Wars" of the 1980s and 1990s—a battle over the educational canon in the humanities. The "Culture Wars" debate—and Bloom's book in particular—highlight some of the most influential beliefs, tensions, and assumptions that have shaped contemporary ideas about intellectualism.

In the "Culture Wars," those on the left supported "opening" the humanities curriculum beyond the traditional canon to include modern issues and texts. Those on the right believed strongly in the basic core curriculum and saw the opening of the curriculum as depleting an important common knowledge among students. A prominent voice for the right, Bloom (a professor of philosophy and political science) framed the literacy and learning crisis in the United States as one in which higher education "closes" rather than "opens" students' minds. According to him, students' minds were being "closed" by an opening of the university curriculum based on modernist sentiments of egalitarianism and cultural relativism. He argued that coupled with cultural forces such as feminism, rock music, the decay of the traditional family, and the sexual revolution, the open curriculum produced students who were more passive and self-centered, less questioning and critical, and less ambitious and passionate. In his words, "Today's select students know so much less, are so much more cut off from the tradition, are so much slacker intellectually, that they make their predecessors look like prodigies of culture" (51). Bloom's critique here exemplifies well the common belief that American society has descended from a previous golden age of intelligence and drive for knowledge to a present age of intellectual apathy, passivity, and ignorance. With its open-or-closed rhetoric, it (like *Anti-intellectualism in American Life*) perpetuated dichotomous thinking about matters of the mind. In this case, U.S. higher education is either *opening* or *closing* young Americans' minds.

For Bloom, the "only serious solution" to the crisis in higher education was to ensure that students at top-tier universities read the Great Books because they engage readers with life's most significant questions (60). He made clear he was not concerned with the "closing" of the minds of *all* students, but with those at the top twenty to thirty universities. The distinction for him was that the purpose of prestigious universities was to provide the best and brightest students a liberal education, while large public colleges were intended "to prepare specialists to meet the practical demands of a complex society" (341). Over the years, Bloom has been labeled elitist because of this distinction and because of his insistence on the superiority of the traditional canon—both of which promote educational hierarchies that limit our views of intellectualism. Intellectualism is for the elite; practical knowledge is for the nonelite. Despite the critiques, Bloom's book and his overarching claim that American higher education was doing more to "close" minds than to "open" them have remained popular, particularly among the public.[2] So too has the tendency for hierarchical views of education, views that deem some knowledge, educational institutions, and motivations for education more valuable than others.

Bloom wasn't the only scholar at that time to lament the loss of "common knowledge" among American students or to equate it with a loss in intellectual development. Journalist and cultural critic Roger Kimball called the broadening of the humanities curriculum a series of "ideologically motivated assaults on the intellectual and moral substance of our culture" (*Tenured Radicals* xvii). Historian Christopher Lasch criticized American educational institutions for a decline in students' knowledge of foreign languages, historical information, and literary classics (*The Culture of Narcissism*) and argued that an absence of common standards leads to "indifference" and "empty minds" (*The Revolt of the Elites* 87). And in his best seller *Cultural Literacy: What Every American Needs to Know,* E. D. Hirsch Jr. blamed the poor state of American education on the absence of a common core of knowledge students needed to be "culturally literate."[3]

Each of these critics claimed that what was ailing the American education system was the absence of particular knowledge—a core or canon of knowledge that includes particular historical and literary knowledge. For Hirsch, it is sufficient for Americans to have *read about,* but not necessarily *read* many of the ideas of the greats of philosophy and literature. For Bloom, however, not only did students need to read the Great Books and read them correctly but they also needed to be students at elite universities. The assertions made in these calls of crisis and decline impose a hierarchy of knowledge that designates some ideas, thinkers, and texts more important and more intellectual than others. They also reinforce the social hierarchies that grant the critics the power to define what knowledge is most important and consequently who should have access to it.

Among the primary critics of efforts to establish a "core curriculum" was Ira Shor, whose argument against it was that it "transmits an official value system disguised as universal knowledge" (*Culture Wars* 23). The decline in students' intellectual ambition, according to Shor, was not the result of a changing "core curriculum" but the consequence of the early 1970s conservative push for careerism, the late 1970s and early 1980s "back-to-the-basics" mentality, and the subsequent push for "excellence" that promoted testing—what he collectively termed the "Conservative Restoration."

The more official response to Bloom's *Closing* was historian Lawrence Levine's *The Opening of the American Mind: Canons, Culture, and History,* published in 1996. Levine countered Bloom's lionization of the Great Books by demonstrating that the traditional canon has evolved over time, reflective of changing social and cultural forces. The "opening" of the modern canon, he argued, was the consequence of society's growing sense of nationalism and multiculturalism and not, as critics claimed, an anti-intellectual downturn in American culture.

The "Culture Wars" debate put the humanities curriculum—and literacy—at the center of public critiques of American higher education and intellectualism. What students should be reading—the traditional canon, or a more multicultural, diverse canon—became the focus of discussions about how to develop students' intellectual abilities and interests. The popularity of Bloom's *Closing* and Hirsch's *Cultural Literacy* in particular convinced the public the United States was experiencing a dangerous "literacy crisis" caused by the loss of a traditional "common knowledge" previously possessed by students. Linking an intellectual, open mind to reading the Great Books or multicultural texts, or to studying a common core of knowledge, these men promoted and worked to institutionalize hierarchies of knowledge. Bloom additionally promoted a hierarchy of educational institutions and a hierarchy of the purpose of education: top-tier colleges produce intellectuals; public colleges produce good citizens and workers. Bloom's best seller, in particular, helped further the belief that a majority of Americans are closed-minded and higher education is responsible for the demise of American thinking. In these ways, the 1980s–90s "Culture Wars" played a significant role in forming contemporary notions of American intellectualism.

THE DUMBEST GENERATION: TWENTY-FIRST-CENTURY CRITIQUES

The indictment that so far best represents twenty-first-century calls of crisis and decline in U.S. literacy and learning is English professor Mark Bauerlein's *The Dumbest Generation*. Exemplified well by Bauerlein's title, the primary injunction against contemporary America is the "dumbing down" of the public, particularly the young. Though contemporary academics, cultural critics, and journalists blame any number of cultural forces for producing "the dumbest generation," the three most prominent ones are technology (particularly digital media and the Internet), a failing education system, and academics' failure to function as public intellectuals who educate and inspire the public. Combined, these critiques highlight the most recent cultural beliefs that contribute to popular exclusionary notions of intellectualism.

How the Digital Age Stupefies Young Americans and Jeopardizes Our Future

The subtitle of Bauerlein's book, *How the Digital Age Stupefies Young Americans and Jeopardizes Our Future (Or, Don't Trust Anyone under 30)* exemplifies well the popular motif that digital technology—and, more specifically, digital literacy practices—are dumbing us down, particularly our young people. As Bauerlein argues, despite an increase in access to information via digital technologies, the average twenty-year-old is abysmally ignorant, unprepared, and apathetic (7–10). His concern—like many others'—is that while current technologies can develop a certain kind of intelligence, they also discourage sustained contemplation and analysis. He disagrees with arguments that young people are benefiting from all the online reading they do, saying the research doesn't yet show this type of literacy is a "full-fledged intellectual practice" (66). He concludes:

> An anti-intellectual outlook prevails in their leisure lives, squashing the lessons of school, and instead of producing a knowledgeable and querulous young mind, the youth culture of American society yields an adolescent consumer enmeshed in juvenile matters and secluded from adult realities. (16)

Bauerlein's indictment of today's youth was informed, at least in part, by his work for the National Endowment for the Arts (NEA). As the organization's director of research and analysis from 2003 to 2005, he contributed to the widely cited 2004 *Reading at Risk* report that once again propagated a "literacy crisis." Based on survey data, the report concluded Americans were reading less and reading less well, and consequently, they were less intellectual and less equipped to be good participatory citizens: "If one believes that active and engaged readers lead richer intellectual lives than non-readers and that a well-read citizenry is essential to a vibrant democracy, the decline of literary reading calls for serious action" (ix). Because the report only counted "literary reading" (defined as the reading of novels, short stories, plays, or poetry) and the reading of "print" texts, it sent the message reading nonliterary and digital texts did not count as "reading"—or, the type of reading that would produce intellectual, engaged citizens. It, in fact, claimed "print culture affords irreplaceable forms of focused attention and contemplation that make complex communications and insights possible. To lose such intellectual capability . . . would constitute a vast cultural impoverishment" and our nation will become "less informed, active, and independent-minded" (vii).

Writer and cultural critic Nicholas Carr voices similar concerns about the influence technology—particularly the Internet—has on reading, writing, and thinking practices. His *Atlantic* article, "Is Google Making Us Stupid?," received much attention when it was published in 2008. His follow-up book, *The Shallows: What the Internet Is Doing to Our Brains*, was an international best seller and a finalist for the 2011 Pulitzer Prize in nonfiction. In both, he argues our interactions with the Internet are changing the way we read and the way we think, making us less patient, less focused, less contemplative readers and thinkers. The consequence of the Internet's "rewiring" of our brains for fast, interrupted engagement with information, he says, is the absence of deep reading, which he equates with deep thinking and a chipping away at the "capacity for concentration and contemplation" needed for reading books, listening to lectures, and writing substantive papers ("Is Google Making Us Stupid?"). "In the choices we have made, consciously or not, about how we use our computers," he argues, "we have rejected the intellectual tradition of solitary, single-minded concentration, the ethic that the book bestowed on us" (*The Shallows* 114). Carr's follow-up to *The Shallows*, *The Glass Cage*, examines more specifically the ways in which automative technologies impair our abilities to think, contemplate, and act.

Another popular critique indicting technology was Susan Jacoby's 2008 *The Age of American Unreason*, a self-proclaimed sequel to Richard Hofstadter's examination of American anti-intellectualism. In her assessment Jacoby argues that in the four decades since Hofstadter's account, America has become "ill with a mutant strain of intertwined ignorance, anti-intellectualism, and anti-rationalism" (xx). A significant part of the problem, she says, is digital and popular media's unremitting stream of images and noises that leave no room for reading and contemplation. In fact, she says, "The more time people spend before the computer screen or any screen, the less time and desire they have for two human activities critical to a fruitful and demanding intellectual life: reading and conversation" (247).

Clear in all of these critiques is a sense that "intellectual life" and "intellectual habits" used to be stronger and that contemporary digital media are paramount among the factors responsible for the decline. These critiques also have in common a linking of literacy (reading in particular) with intellectualism. Bauerlein claims research doesn't yet show online reading is a "full-fledged intellectual practice." The NEA claims readers of literary texts have greater "intellectual capability" and lead "richer intellectual lives." Carr credits the book with "the intellectual tradition of solitary, single-minded concentration." And Jacoby argues reading and conversation are critical to "a fruitful and demanding intellectual life." Combined, they associate the reading of "print" texts with concentration, conversation, and contemplation; in return, they associate digital literacy with the absence or decline of these "intellectual capabilities." These widespread and popular beliefs reinforce narrow notions of intellectualism by connecting it with traditional book reading and linking anti- or nonintellectualism with digital literacy.

Such beliefs perpetuate a "myth of decline [of literacy]" (Graff, "The Literacy Myth at Thirty"). This myth, Harvey J. Graff contends, "neglects the changing modes of communication, and in particular the increasing importance of media that do not depend completely on print"—resulting in a "powerful variant" of the literacy myth (640). The literacy myth, as Graff defined it, is the belief that the acquisition of literacy by itself is necessary for—and necessarily leads to—economic, social, and cognitive advancement (*The Literacy Myth* xxxvi–xxxviii). In this case, contemporary rhetoric sends the message that the acquisition or practice of *some literacies* (for instance, book, print, and literary reading) are necessary for and necessarily result in intellectual development and that other literacies (digital literacies in particular) necessarily lead to intellectual decline.

While some cultural critics have recently published counterarguments to the many crisis-infused critiques of technology's influence on our minds (Steven Johnson's *Everything Bad Is Good for You: How Today's Popular Culture Is Actually Making Us Smarter,* Marc Prensky's *Brain Gain: Technology and the Quest for Digital Wisdom,* Clive Thompson's *Smarter Than You Think: How Technology Is Changing Our Minds for the Better,* and James Paul Gee's *The Anti-Education Era: Creating Smarter Students through Digital Learning*), the critiques damning technology are much more popular and pervasive. And interestingly, though Gee's book ends by highlighting ways Americans can use technology to "get smart before it's too late," the majority of the book discusses the ways in which technology has made us "stupid."

Considering side-by-side the rhetoric of popular texts examining technology's effects on the mind, it is clear that contemporary critiques further the dichotomous thinking about literacy, learning, and intellectualism we saw in Hofstadter's and Bloom's work. In this case, critics claim that Americans are either *smart* or *dumb.* And, they conclude, most are dumb. As H. L. Mencken once wrote, "No one ever went broke underestimating the intelligence of the American public." And as English professor William Pannapacker recently wrote, "Several generations later, one might speculate that no publisher has ever lost money with a book accusing Americans—particularly young ones—of being stupid."[4] To be clear, it remains popular and profitable to malign the American mind and encourage limited, reductive understandings of American intellectualism.

Academically Adrift

A second theme among twenty-first-century critiques of American literacy and learning is that our schools increasingly fail to promote and foster intellectual growth. The critiques blame the "corporatization" of higher education and the emphasis on testing and assessment in primary and secondary schools. The tension present in these discussions highlights the ongoing cultural conflict over the purpose of education: should schools focus on making students "college and career ready," or on developing students' ways of thinking and learning? The responses typically take a dichotomous view: schools exist to do one or the other, not both. And the problem, critics contend, is our educational policies and reforms consistently steer educational institutions toward the former. This debate over the purpose of education and institutions' actions toward meeting that purpose informs contemporary views of intellectualism because it concerns the primary institutions assumed to cultivate American intellectualism.

A recent and apt metaphor for contemporary critiques of American higher education is the one provided by the highly publicized *Academically Adrift: Limited Learning on College Campuses.*[5] The authors, sociologists Richard Arum and Josipa Roska, assert that while more and more students are going to college and paying high costs for it, many experience little to no improvement in "critical thinking, complex reasoning, and written communication" (121). Consequently, the authors argue, higher education renders students "adrift" in college and (as Arum and Roska contend in their follow-up book *Aspiring Adults Adrift*) when they leave school and attempt to enter the workforce. The problem, they insist, is universities have a "market-based logic of education" and lack rigor (16); they also blame faculty and administrators for moving away from their roles as supporters of students' academic development (127). While their study has been widely cited, critics have found fault with their use of the Collegiate Learning Assessment (CLA)[6] exam, with the "time period" of assessment (from students' first semester to their third, not their final), and with their definition of "writing." Nonetheless, their assessment of higher education has fueled public concern about the intellectual contributions of American colleges.

Arum and Roska's study is just one of the prominent criticisms of higher education in recent years, many of which have faulted the "corporatization" of universities for students' lack of knowledge, their apathy, and a loss of development of critical thinking and intellectual engagement. The problem, most argue, is that corporate attitudes result in high costs for students, low wages and poor conditions for faculty, the treatment of students as consumers, and curriculum decisions based on cost-effectiveness and student retention (Bousquet, Donoghue, Edmundson, Giroux). In Henry A. Giroux's words, "many institutions of higher education are now committed almost exclusively to economic growth, instrumental rationality, and preparing students for the workforce" ("The Disappearing Intellectual" 166). According to William

Deresiewicz, the problem extends to America's elite universities which force students to "choose between learning and success" (4).

The central concern about primary and secondary education's influence on literacy and learning in the United States is the recent emphasis on assessment and testing, which many argue has stifled—rather than fostered—intellectual curiosity. One of the most widely read education scholars, Diane Ravitch, argues that because of the emphasis on basic skills and improved test scores, the No Child Left Behind (NCLB) curriculum "produced mountains of data, not educated citizens," ignoring the significance of attaining knowledge and promoting "a cramped, mechanistic, profoundly anti-intellectual definition of education" (29). In short, she claims, "By our current methods, we may be training (not educating) a generation of children who are repelled by learning, thinking that it means only drudgery, worksheets, test preparation, and test-taking" (231).

The new Common Core State Standards (CCSS) have a similar emphasis on testing and on "college and career readiness" that Ravitch and others fear will only perpetuate the problem. For example, while some may argue the standards' focus on evidence-based, argumentative and informative (and not just narrative) writing, along with their attention to purpose and audience, are improvements over previous writing standards and may more likely foster students' critical thinking and intellectual development, as Linda Adler-Kassner has argued, these standards are being implemented—and sold to the public—in service of a vocationally oriented view of education. In other words, though the standards may include critical thinking as a goal, the skills they are teaching are being packaged and sold as skills necessary for equipping students to be economically competitive citizens rather than independent, engaged thinkers ("The Companies We Keep"). In fact, the CCSS Initiative, in its own words, states the standards were "designed to ensure students are prepared for today's entry-level careers, freshman-level college courses, and workforce training programs" (*Common Core State Standards*). Such rhetoric sends a clear message: the purpose of K–12 education is to prepare young Americans to be workers, not thinkers.

If these critiques are correct, American schools at all levels promote and perpetuate non- and anti-intellectual attitudes toward learning. The pervasiveness of these critiques damages the public's faith in schools and, as Mike Rose contends, can lead to less funding or support for education (*Back to School* 16). These critiques also affect Americans' notions of what it means to be educated. For example, if colleges are consistently berated for failing to meet their intellectual vision, students and parents lower their expectations and (as my own students' comments demonstrate) move away from viewing college as a time and space for intellectual development. Consequently, students and the public at large fail to see schools as intellectual communities the public can participate in. In other words, they disassociate American public education from American intellectualism.

Public Intellectuals: A Study of Decline

Higher education has also been implicated in the "dumbing down" (or decline) of American culture through the many incantations that academics are not successfully serving as public intellectuals who educate and inspire the public. Originally documented by historian Russell Jacoby in *The Last Intellectuals*,[7] the "decline of the public intellectual" is a recurring theme in contemporary crisis rhetoric that influences greatly how "intellectual" and "intellectualism" get defined. Primary among the critiques is Richard A. Posner's *Public Intellectuals: A Study of Decline*. Posner claims that there aren't necessarily fewer public intellectuals (as the title might imply), but that they are increasingly academics who do not adequately play the role of "critical commentator addressing a nonspecialist audience on matters of broad public concern" (5). Overall, he claims, the significance and contributions of public intellectuals (or academics) is "deteriorating" (6). Henry A. Giroux's view is that most academics aren't functioning as public intellectuals either because they don't see a need to address the public or take on social issues, or because their working conditions don't allow it ("Noam Chomsky").

While Posner's and Giroux's reviews exemplify well the numerous critiques of academics' failure to serve as public intellectuals, other participants in the discussion focus on "calling" academics to become productive public intellectuals. Among the most recent of these calls was an article in *Academe* by three rhetoric and composition professors (Nicholas Behm, Sherry Rankins-Robertson, and Duane Roen). In "The Case for Academics as Public Intellectuals," the authors argue that particularly because politicians are failing to adequately address issues of public concern, academics need to "collaborate with the public to address society's core challenges." Rather than view their role as public intellectuals as merely disseminating their knowledge to a "dependent" and "passive" public (as some have interpreted it), they need to work *with* the public, demonstrating higher education can play an important role in "the democratic work of the country."

While the sentiment that academics should make their research accessible to the public and connect it to issues of public concern is a positive one, these calls for academics to be public intellectuals also position academics as the primary arbiters of intellectualism. Once again, this conflation of intellectual and academic limits Americans' views of intellectualism and their understanding of who can engage in intellectual work. (Noted earlier, many of my students' drawings of intellectualism depicted professors.) In addition, such calls position the public as passive consumers and presume the knowledge of academics is more valuable than the public's own knowledge, or that scholarly knowledge is more valuable than experiential, nonscholarly knowledge. Combined, these critiques reinforce popular images of intellectuals as professors who serve as the gatekeepers to American intellectualism.

CONSEQUENCES AND CONTRIBUTIONS

As this survey shows, the calls of crisis and decline in American literacy and learning since Hofstadter's declaration are widespread and damning. They highlight and provide evidence of the very real challenges Americans face today: young Americans often lack knowledge about significant dates, historical events, texts, etc. and have increasingly consumerist and careerist views of education; recent education reforms that value testing and prioritize the production of good workers disassociate American education from intellectual curiosity and development; technology and other media can foster literacy practices that decrease concentration or contemplation; and academics don't consistently communicate or work with the public. The rhetoric used to discuss these issues, however, perpetuates narrow notions of intellectualism that equate it with living a "life of the mind," with academics and academic success, or with studying "highbrow" ideas at elite institutions of higher education. It also reinforces educational hierarchies that privilege the knowledge, learning sites, and educational experiences of the cultural elite and promotes a variation of the literacy myth that influences the public's expectations for and engagement with literacy.

The titles of the three primary texts at the center of these critiques exemplify well the change in crisis rhetoric over time. *Anti-intellectualism in American Life* implies an existence or presence of anti-intellectualism in American beliefs about learning and education. The use of the gerund in *The Closing of the American Mind* denotes something is happening, or perhaps changing: the minds of Americans are in the process of closing. In contrast, the use of the superlative in *The Dumbest Generation* evokes finitude, finality. The damage has been done: Americans are the dumbest they have ever been. Collectively, these texts send the message that while America has always had an anti-intellectual leaning, it has been on a continuous and destructive descent into the present state of ubiquitous intellectual apathy and ignorance.

These central texts also highlight the cultural tendency for dichotomous thinking about education and intellectualism: intellectual/anti-intellectual; open mind/closed mind; smart/dumb. This type of thinking severely limits what knowledge, activities, educational institutions, and people fall under the rubric of intellectual. For instance, if only "highbrow" knowledge is considered intellectual, then knowledge considered practical, useful, or experiential is devalued or classified nonintellectual. Or, if only higher-ranking academic institutions are thought to open minds, then the learning that takes place at vocational, technical, or nontraditional sites of learning is associated with closing minds. And if particular literacy practices such as the reading of literary texts, the Great Books, or print texts are believed to make us smart, then the basic, nonliterary, and digital literacies central to the work of rhetoric, composition, and literacy studies are assumed to dumb us down. This dichotomous and hierarchical view hampers our ability to recognize, evaluate, and celebrate a broad range of intellectual activities and educational institutions that are often accessible to nonelite populations—activities and institutions this book seeks to showcase.

Because this rhetoric influences what literacy practices get valued and taught, how they are measured, and the public's—and our students'—engagement with them, the stakes are high for rhetoric, composition, and literacy studies scholars. Despite what's at stake, a review of the last decade of research in the field shows that while we have engaged in productive discussions and debates about the three prominent contemporary issues subsumed in this crisis rhetoric (digital literacy, the problem with recent education "reforms," and public intellectualism), we have paid little attention to their connection to the causes and consequences of narrow notions of intellectualism.

A search of several of the top journals in the field[8] reveals the rhetoric of anti-intellectualism in American culture has been referenced only a few times in the last decade. In 2005, Susan Kates pointed out we live in a "fiercely anti-intellectual atmosphere" that poses significant challenges to civic discourse and taints the public's view of academics in the humanities. Consequently, she argued, we need do a better job of communicating in dialogue with the public ("Emerging Technologies" 383). More recently, Susan Searls Giroux published "The Age of Unreason: Race and the Drama of American Anti-Intellectualism" in the *Journal of Advanced Composition*. In it, she argues that the anti-intellectualism Hofstadter wrote about prevails and drives a new "colorblind" racism that gives the illusion that we are a raceless society and therefore encourages the public to overlook its problematic persistence. Similarly, a search of the last decade of catalogs for the *Conference on College Composition and Communication* (CCCC) shows that only one talk has referenced the term *anti-intellectual* in its title ("Exploring the Anti-intellectual Rhetoric of Creationism").

Debates about digital literacy and digital pedagogies have been forefront in the field's research in the past decade, though not in relation to reductive notions of intellectualism. Cynthia L. Selfe's call at the turn of the century for scholar-teachers to "pay attention" to the prominent cultural narratives that position technology as *either* harmful *or* beneficial to literacy practices resulted in more awareness of the influence public rhetoric can have on the public's understanding of technology and its relationship to literacy (25). Jason Palmeri's recent history of multimodal writing pedagogy makes clear, though, that these same narratives have persisted within the field itself, with some scholars assuming electronic forms of composing are harmful for students' development as critical writers and thinkers and others assuming they are inherently beneficial for students (11). Demonstrations of technology's intellectual benefits have been highlighted several times at CCCC in the past decade, with talk and panel titles including "Net Work: The Intellectual, Social, and Material Function of Networks in the Composing Process," "Facebook and the Gramscian Organic Intellectual," and "Just Because It Is Hands-On Doesn't Meant It's Not Intellectual: The Knowledge-Building Work of Multimedia Production Practices." Once again, there's no evidence the field has connected its own investment in digital literacies with the calls of crisis and decline that perpetuate the notion digital literacies have contributed much to American intellectual apathy.

Linda Adler-Kassner has been prominent among rhetoric and composition scholars participating in discussions about recent education reforms and their influence on the work of our field. In a 2010 article in *College Composition and Communication*, she and Susanmarie Harrington warned that the message recent education reforms send is that the purpose of education is to prepare students to become workers. The writing skills seen as valuable toward that end are, most often, grammatical correctness and the ability to reproduce "particular interpretations or modes" (95). As they note, the literacy practices we associate with the development of critical thinking and learning are devalued and receive less support. More recently, several scholars in the field responded to *Academically Adrift*. Some praised the authors for bringing to the forefront the issue of student learning on college campuses and for associating that learning with writing and critical thinking. The text was criticized, however, for its methodology and reliance on a problematic testing tool (Rankins-Robertson et al; "Reviews"). In addition to these contributions, Mike Rose has argued that what we need to do in response to reform efforts' emphasis on testing and economic competitiveness is to change how we talk about school. What we need, he claims, is

> public talk that links education to a more decent, thoughtful, open society. Talk that raises in us as a people the appreciation for deliberation and reflection, or for taking intellectual risks and thinking widely—for the sheer power and pleasure of using our minds, alone or in concert with others. (*Why School?* 4; 28)

The subject of public intellectualism has been discussed several times at CCCC in the past decade. Based on the presentation and panel titles, these discussions centered on one of two things: framing the work of the field as public intellectualism or teaching practices designed to help students function as public intellectuals. The definition of public intellectualism in both appears to be "writing for the public." A number of recent books and articles also demonstrate the field's interest in public intellectualism. In addition to the *Academe* article by Behm, Rankins-Robertson, and Roen mentioned earlier, Kates has called us to use "emerging technologies" to engage in public intellectualism, Adler-Kassner has argued that we need to help shape the public's perceptions of our work by engaging the public (*The Activist WPA*), and Christian Weisser has argued that we need to assume the role of "activist intellectual." And most recently, Samuel McCormick encouraged us to examine the rhetorical strategies of intellectuals engaging in more subtle—and yet powerful—forms of public advocacy (*Letters to Power*).

Combined, the above discussions make clear these issues are important to the field. However, they fail to connect them substantively to limited notions of intellectualism that position much of the public, many of our students, and some of the work we do as non- or anti-intellectual. *Reimagining Popular Notions of American Intellectualism* builds on these conversations in productive and meaningful ways. In response to Rose's call for "public talk" that associates education with reflection, deliberation, and pleasurable intellectual work, this books reimagines intellectualism so it lauds an interest in, appreciation for, and engagement with learning, knowledge, deliberation, critical thinking, and inquiry irrespective of the particular knowledge, texts, or institutions a person engages with. By placing the emphasis on a person's attitude toward learning and his or her engagement with ideas, we can expand the learners and sites of learning we recognize as intellectual—contesting the elitist notion that a majority of Americans are ignorant and anti-intellectual and that the United States is void of intellectuals and intellectualism outside its elite universities. In this way, the book works to refocus the discussion of "public intellectualism" from calls for academics to communicate with the public to recognizing the public's own intellectual work. And like Selfe's and Palmeri's calls for teachers to aid students in developing a "critical technological literacy" that helps them understand and challenge the assumptions made about their own and their culture's interactions with digital media, this book calls us to aid students in understanding and challenging the influence of the rhetoric of anti-intellectualism and ignorance in their interactions not only with digital media but also with their literacy and educational experiences at large.

In the case studies that follow, I reexamine the literacy and learning practices of three nontraditional sites of education in the United States through the lens of the more expansive and democratic definition of intellectualism I propose. I do this to demonstrate concretely that despite longstanding cultural beliefs that limit who and what fall under the rubric of intellectualism, many adult learners *have* engaged and *do* engage in the type of intellectual work we value in our discussions of the purpose and rewards of education. More specifically, these case studies work to contest assumptions that the study of useful knowledge, education for a practical purpose, basic literacy education, adult education in general, and education at nonelite institutions have not fostered—or cannot foster—intellectualism among the American public.

chapter two

INTELLECTUALISM AND THE DIFFUSION OF USEFUL KNOWLEDGE

The Nineteenth-Century American Lyceum

STARTED AT A TIME WHEN American society believed in and actively sought self-improvement through the acquisition of "useful knowledge," the American lyceum[1] was established in 1826 by educator and science enthusiast Josiah Holbrook.[2] His goal was to make accessible to the public "practical scientific instruction" and other "useful knowledge." Early lyceums were small, local community associations that met weekly to hear local experts speak on a variety of subjects or to engage in discussions and debates about proposed topics. By 1845 the lyceum had become primarily a popular lecture circuit. After the Civil War it transformed once again—this time into a travelling show that included lectures but also a variety of entertainers.

While scholars have credited the American lyceum with increasing the public's access to information and with serving as an important forum for public education and influential rhetoric (Bode, Ray, Hayes, Horner, Noffsinger, Johnson, Stambler, Mead, Scott), because its mission was to disseminate useful knowledge for the purpose of practical application to daily life it has not fallen under the rubric of intellectualism as it is today defined. This mission (noted earlier) has traditionally been associated with non- or anti-intellectualism. Additionally, the lyceum has been viewed by some as a "consensus builder" that transmitted facts from the learned to the less learned and criticized by others for its post–Civil War transformation into a platform for entertainment.

This chapter reevaluates the lyceum's contributions to public intellectualism in the nineteenth century, drawing heavily on archival documents that provide insight into the purpose of the lyceum, the useful knowledge it disseminated, the literacy and learning practices it nurtured, its postwar transformation, and the access it provided to knowledge and education. The archival research here intentionally spans the scope and development of the lyceum, drawing not only from Holbrook's initial writings but also from town meeting minutes and records, lectures, newspaper reports, advertisements, and lyceum periodicals. Building on existing scholarship (much of which focuses on eastern lyceums), this chapter surveys previously unexamined archives from Ohio lyceums that provide a closer look at the institution in practice as it materialized outside the original organizations started on the East Coast.

Based on this archival work and the work of previous lyceum scholars, I argue that in its dissemination of useful knowledge for practical application, the lyceum fostered a thirst for knowledge among participants and promoted intellectual inquiry and deliberation. It is important to recognize the intellectual import of this work because it shines light on the nineteenth-century American public's interest in, appreciation for, and engagement with knowledge, learning, deliberation, critical thinking, and inquiry. These findings not only make clear that narrow, exclusionary notions of intellectualism have concealed (and devalued) the knowledge and learning and literacy practices of nonelite populations but they also demonstrate the value in mindfully reconsidering what it means to participate in intellectual activity.

THE LYCEUM AND NINETEENTH-CENTURY ADULT EDUCATION

Nineteenth-century Americans valued the acquisition of knowledge because they believed it had the potential to improve an individual's morality, taste, character, and mind. In response to the public's interest in self-improvement and the acquisition of knowledge, the United States experienced a significant increase in the founding of adult education societies focused on spreading useful knowledge from the late eighteenth century to the mid-nineteenth century (Brown, "The Emergence" 64–65). In fact, by the early 1830s there were hundreds of subscription reading rooms and libraries, debating clubs, and associations that sponsored lectures (Grattan 154).[3] Among the most popular adult education societies of the time was the American lyceum.[4]

From its inception, the lyceum quickly spread, especially in New England,[5] with branches numbering around one hundred in 1828 and three thousand by 1834 (Noffsinger 101). Lyceums were popular during this time because of the low cost, the public's interest in education, the desire for personal improvement, the relative absence of other forms of amusement, the recent increase in literacy, and the promotion of lyceums through newspapers and magazines (Bode 27–35). As lyceums became more popular, they transformed into a public lecture circuit (around 1845). At first lectures were still organized by local associations, but they included nationally known traveling speakers like Ralph Waldo Emerson, Henry D. Thoreau, and Oliver Wendell Holmes. Lecture topics included varied subjects and issues of the time. There is some discrepancy among scholars about who actually attended lyceum meetings and lectures, and it most certainly varied among communities. The stated intention, however, was for lyceums to be open to all citizens, regardless of class or access to more traditional educational institutions. In Holbrook's words, lyceums should "diffuse the greatest quantity of useful information among the various classes of the community" ("Associations" 596).

Though the lyceum all but disappeared during the Civil War, it gained popularity after the war with high-paid popular lecturers like Wendell Phillips, William Lloyd Garrison, Henry Ward Beecher, Susan B. Anthony, and Julia Ward Howe participating in traveling groups organized, advertised, and produced by lyceum bureaus. These travelling groups centered on lectures, but also included dramatic and musical performances and other entertainment. This new lyceum reached its peak in popularity between 1875 and 1900 (with audiences of approximately 5 million people a year). Between 1920 and 1930, the American lyceum began to dissipate due to the development of radio and film, the increased availability of newspapers and magazines, and the popularity of the opera house (Brigance 127).

THE PURPOSE OF THE LYCEUM

Holbrook believed, like the nineteenth-century public, that knowledge could improve an individual's "moral and intellectual taste." He described his vision for the lyceum in an 1826 article in the *American Journal of Education* (*AJE*)[6]:

> It seems to me that if associations for mutual instruction in the sciences and other branches of useful knowledge, could once be started in our villages, and upon a general plan, they would increase with great rapidity, and do more for the general diffusion of knowledge, and for raising the moral and intellectual taste of our countrymen, than any other expedient which can possibly be devised. And it may be questioned if there is any other way, to check the progress of that monster, intemperance, which is making such havoc with talents, morals, and every thing that raises man above the brute, but by presenting some object of sufficient interest to divert the attention of the young from places and practices which lead to dissipation and to ruin. ("Associations" 594–96)

For Holbrook, the intellectual and moral benefits of the lyceum were intertwined; he saw among the advantages of disseminating information to the public dissuading "that monster, intemperance." His list of objectives for these "mutual instruction societies" in the same document prioritizes the education aspect of his vision: "to procure for youths an economical and practical education," "to diffuse rational and useful information through the community generally," and "to apply the sciences and the various branches of education to the domestic and useful arts, and to all the common purposes of life" ("Associations" 595).

As his vision and objectives demonstrate, Holbrook designed the lyceum to improve education and spread practical knowledge the public could apply in their daily lives. Because contemporary narrow notions of intellectualism associate it with a "life of the mind" and distinguish it from learning for practical purposes or practical application, the practical bent of the lyceum is the primary reason it has been overlooked in discussions of American intellectualism.

To better understand what Holbrook believed were the intellectual benefits of the lyceum, it is important to examine his use of the word *intellectual* in its historical context. The *Oxford English Dictionary* (OED) indicates *intellect* was commonly used in the nineteenth century to refer to someone possessing understanding or intelligence, and to refer to "that faculty, or sum of faculties, of the mind or soul by which one knows and reasons (excluding sensation, and sometimes imagination; distinguished from *feeling* and *will*); power of thought; understanding." The *OED* notes *intellectual* was used in the nineteenth century to mean "possessing a high degree of understanding; given to pursuits that exercise the intellect" and "that appeals to or engages the intellect; requiring the exercise of understanding."

Holbrook's use of the word *intellectual* in his 1826 proclamation for the lyceum is consistent with the *OED*'s description of nineteenth-century use of the term. In the passage quoted above, Holbrook expresses his hope that the lyceum could help raise *intellectual taste*. He uses the word again when he lists what scientific subjects lyceums should discuss and then adds "or any political, intellectual, or moral subject" ("Associations" 595). Later in the article Holbrook writes that the associations he is proposing may help in establishing institutions "for giving to youths a thorough education, intellectual, moral and physical" (595). And finally, he proposes having general or state boards for these associations for the purpose of devising and recommending a system of education "to secure to the rising generation the best intellectual, moral, and physical education" (596). Consistent with common usage of the term in the nineteenth century, Holbrook appears to be using *intellectual* as a synonym for intelligence or mental faculties. From this we can glean that for Holbrook, the intellectual purpose of the lyceum was to increase knowledge, reason, and understanding—not to foster "the life of the mind" or to spread "highbrow" knowledge to the elite among the population (as the term gets used now).

Archival documents from local Ohio lyceums affirm that the intellectual vision Holbrook had was shared by other organizations and their leaders. For example, Cincinnati Law School professor Timothy Walker, in an 1830 address at the opening of the Charlestown (Ohio) Lyceum, declared,

> To organize a Lyceum, is merely to provide a reservoir of knowledge. To fill this reservoir there should be streams flowing into it from every quarter. In plain language, the members must in their turn become teachers of themselves and of each other. (7)

According to the Constitution of the Williams Lyceum Society of Ohio, "The object of this Society shall be the mutual improvement of all its members in the investigation and communication of truth by means of public speaking" (Minute Book, 1844–46). Similarly, the South Charleston (Ohio) Lyceum declared in its Preamble, "We the undersigned, desirous of securing to ourselves the advantages of mutual improvement by means of debates, lectures, essays, declamations, music, etc. resolve to organize an association and adopt the following Constitution" (Records, 1867–71).

These documents reveal that for Holbrook and other lyceum leaders, among the primary purposes of the lyceum was an intellectual one, which at the time was to disseminate useful knowledge to improve understanding and reasoning. Considering the examples come from Holbrook in 1826, a speech in 1830, a minute book dated 1844–46, and meeting records dated 1867–71, there is some evidence the intellectual objectives Holbrook conceived for the lyceum were present in different forms of the lyceum over time. These archival documents also reveal that the nineteenth-century lyceum was not intended to cultivate intellectualism as it is now defined; it was not disseminating highbrow knowledge or promoting a "life of the mind." If we reimagine intellectualism as this book proposes, however, it is possible to recognize the lyceum's role in fostering intellectualism among the nineteenth-century public.

THE DIFFUSION OF USEFUL KNOWLEDGE

The lyceum's emphasis on useful knowledge is the primary characteristic that casts it as a nonintellectual educational institution. Looking closely at what knowledge was considered "useful" by Holbrook and other lyceum leaders in the nineteenth century and also what knowledge was actually disseminated by nineteenth-century lyceums challenges the assumption that knowledge deemed "useful" cannot promote or cultivate intellectual engagement and inquiry.

According to nineteenth-century lyceum documents, lyceum leaders conceived of useful knowledge broadly, evidenced by their descriptions of useful knowledge and by the variety of subjects considered appropriate for lyceums. In his inaugural address for the Mount Vernon (Ohio) Lyceum, Henry Barnes Curtis (a lawyer and president of this lyceum branch) stated that in the dissemination of useful knowledge, lyceums "are not limited to books, and scholastic researches, in the *useful operations* of our society; but they extend to all the common transactions of life" (4–5). Timothy Walker, in his 1830 address to the Charlestown Lyceum, described useful knowledge this way:

> Useful knowledge is what we look for in Lyceums; not brilliancy, not wit. Sparkling genius will avail us far less than unpolished common sense. Practical information is what the many want, such information as they can turn to useful account in the daily concerns of life. To furnish this, at the cheapest possible rate, is what I understand to be the design of this, and all similar associations. (5–6)

Useful knowledge, as described by Curtis and Walker, is broadly conceived, with the main criteria being its applicability or utility. Their definition of useful knowledge is consistent with the nineteenth-century definition of *useful*: "Having the character or quality to be of use or utility; suitable for use; advantageous, profitable, beneficial" (*OED*). Evident in Walker's comments is also the desire to distinguish between brilliance and possession of useful knowledge and between genius and common sense. This distinction seems akin to more contemporary desires to be seen as intelligent but not as intellectual, indicating that perhaps the stigma of brilliance and intellectualism is a longstanding one in American culture.

We get a clearer picture of what knowledge was considered useful from the specific topics lyceums tackled. In his 1826 proclamation for the establishment of lyceums, Holbrook lists the following subjects as the types of knowledge lyceums should disseminate: history, chemistry, mechanics, botany, mathematics, political economy, "or any political, intellectual, or moral subject" ("Associations" 595). Curtis listed as important for lyceums philosophy, chemistry, botany, literature, and belles letters. With an emphasis on scientific subjects, a wide array of topics was considered suitable for lyceums.

Lyceum records and documents reveal the subjects covered by lyceums were broad not only in theory but also in practice. This is true for both local lyceum meetings and lyceum public lectures, and also for lyceum periodicals published in the 1830s to disseminate useful knowledge in written form. The following is a partial list of topics discussed and debated at the meetings of local lyceum organizations in Ohio between 1842 and 1871.[7]

- Ought a member of our state or national legislature to obey the will of his constituents so far as to vote contrary to his own judgment?
- Would it be good policy by legal enactment to prevent any of the two proffessions [*sic*] Law or Medicine from practicing without a diploma?
- Would it be expedient for the Legislature of Ohio to establish a school library at each school district in the state?
- Resolved that oratory has done more to secure the votes of the people than Arms.
- Resolved that the northern part of these United States would be justifiable in separating from the southern part.
- Resolved that lawers [*sic*] are more useful to community than Doctors.
- Resolved that the female should have equal privileges with the male in the exercise of the elective franchise and governmental affairs.
- Resolved that capital punishment should be abolished.

This list demonstrates that useful knowledge included social, cultural, and political issues of the time—issues that would likely have incited some deliberation, discussion, and critical thinking.

Lyceum lectures also covered a range of subjects. According to literary historian Carl Bode, a lyceum lecture series in Salem, Massachusetts, in 1838–39 included general informative speeches about the sun, the honey bee, and instinct but also more complex topics like the causes of the American Revolution, the rights of women, and education (48). Similarly, historian Donald Scott notes that during its 1851–52 season, the lyceum in Belfast, Maine, had lectures on astronomy, biology, and physiology, but also the equality of the human condition and the true mission of women (792). The focus of Theodore Sedgwick's 1831 lecture to a Massachusetts lyceum was, "Is it possible to abolish African Slavery in this country; or, in other words, is the perpetual subjugation of the African race the necessary result of the condition of human nature?" (2). Sedgwick recognized the "usefulness" of this subject, calling it "perhaps, the most momentous [question] that concerns the human race" (2).

Holbrook started two lyceum periodicals to enact the mission of lyceums, but in written form. These periodicals also encompassed a variety of topics. Started in 1831, *Scientific Tracts*[8] focused on scientific subjects, including the atmosphere, geology, heat, entomology, weather, the eye, sound, meteors, and electricity. Each edition consisted of a general description of the topic, definitions of important terms and concepts, and sometimes included drawings and diagrams to ease understanding. *Family Lyceum*[9] was a four-page weekly general-knowledge journal started by Holbrook that lasted from mid-1832 to late 1833. Like *Scientific Tracts, Family Lyceum* included scientific subjects such as biology, chemistry, geology, forestry, and meteorology. It covered them in less depth though (usually only a few paragraphs) and also dealt with subjects like intellects, morals, and the different types and locations of lyceums.

These lists of questions, topics, and issues covered by lyceum meetings, lyceum lectures, and lyceum periodicals show the wide range of knowledge recognized as useful and practical in the nineteenth century. The only criterion seems to be usefulness in daily life; the actual topics and issues could vary widely. In fact, Scott has claimed that Americans who attended public lectures in the nineteenth century believed "almost all knowledge was potentially useful" (801).

The inclusion of such a wide range of subjects also demonstrates that the nineteenth-century concept of *useful* was not just useful in the form of daily physical activities, but also in the form of social and civic actions and in the development of ideas and opinions. Historian C. Hartley Grattan noted, "The Lyceums were largely concerned with knowledge that was 'useful' but not necessarily vocational" (155). In other words, the information the lyceum disseminated could be useful in the operation of the hand *and* in the operation of the mind. For example, the description of forest trees in the eighth edition of *Scientific Tracts* would be useful for identifying, using, and appreciating a variety of trees, while Sedgwick's 1831 lecture on slavery would have been useful in participants' understanding of the issue of slavery and would most likely have influenced their opinions about the issue. In addition, the Williams Lyceum Society of Greenfield Academy's discussion about whether or not the North should secede from the Union (Minute Book) would have been useful in forming opinions, and possibly in participants' social and political actions. Sometimes these subjects of various "uses" were even located side by side. For example, the July 28, 1832, edition of *Family Lyceum* contained short descriptions of heat, combustion, and oxygen alongside a discussion of schools in the United States that raised the question of whether or not teachers are qualified and whether or not students are taught well.

Another issue relevant to the intellectual import of the content of lyceums is the extent to which each subject was covered. Because the lyceum's goal was to spread knowledge about many subjects, the emphasis for lyceum lectures, discussions, and articles was on breadth, not depth. For example, *Family Lyceum* articles were only a few paragraphs in length. Although *Scientific Tracts*' articles were more extensive (devoting twenty to twenty-five pages for each topic), they were still relatively brief. In addition, lyceum meeting discussions were typically contained to one meeting. And, lyceum lectures were usually less than an hour long. Communications professor Angela G. Ray referred to the lyceum's emphasis on breadth over depth as an effort to make Americans "generalists," not "specialists" (181). According to Scott, though, no matter what the subject, nineteenth-century audiences expected lecturers to do more than describe a subject; they were expected to place the topic in "a broad, interpretive context" and leave them feeling they had an "enlarged understanding" rather than merely basic comprehension of a subject (803–6). Because the definition of intellectualism proposed in this book is primarily concerned with the audience's interest in and critical engagement with the knowledge disseminated, an emphasis on breadth over depth does not take away from the intellectual influence an educational institution can have on participants. Therefore, the lyceum's emphasis on breadth over depth does not relegate its work nonintellectual.

It is important to acknowledge here that what Ray and Scott have argued complicates the lyceum's role as disseminator of knowledge to the nineteenth-century public. In her analysis of the lyceum, Ray argued that because white, male, New England Protestants were in charge of most of the lyceums, they served as the gatekeepers of the content (or useful knowledge) disseminated. In her words, "This idea of public education restricted systematic learning and scholarship to an authoritative elite and thus reinforced the cultural power of that class" (17). And because the lyceum also had the objective of moral improvement, those in charge had the power to define that too. Scott has contended, however, that the audience had some control over the content of lectures because "lecturers who could not attract a large enough audience did not remain popular lecturers for very long, and societies that failed to provide a course of sufficient popularity also had trouble surviving" (807). If, though, as Scott has stated, the "public" the lyceum lectures served by the 1850s was primarily white, Anglo-Saxon middle-class Protestants in the north (809), then control was still in the hands of the same group of people. Understanding who had primary control over what knowledge was disseminated and deemed "useful" is important because it does show that with the objective of educating "the various classes of the community," the lyceum still reinforced the power of a particular class—an issue that remains today.

Recognizing the lyceum perpetuated some class privilege, this examination of the content of lyceums nevertheless challenges contemporary assumptions that an emphasis on useful knowledge negates an institution's ability to foster learners' intellectualism. Because knowledge was seen as useful in a broad sense, lyceums disseminated a wide variety of knowledge useful both abstractly and concretely. By spreading useful knowledge, lyceums also could have interested people in subjects they had known little or nothing about, given people foundational knowledge they could build on, and stimulated their minds and their curiosity. These achievements, along with the learning activities lyceums promoted and fostered, make the lyceum not only a "disseminator of useful knowledge" but also a potential sponsor of intellectualism.

LITERACY AND LEARNING PRACTICES PROMOTED BY THE LYCEUM

In his 1826 proclamation of his vision for the lyceum, Holbrook made clear he did not intend lyceums to disseminate useful knowledge to a passive, unengaged audience. Rather, Holbrook intended participants to share their expertise with each other and to discuss, examine, debate, and investigate further the information they gained. In Holbrook's words, "The society will hold meetings, as often as they think it expedient, for the purpose of mutual instruction in the sciences, by investigating and discussing them or any other branch of useful knowledge" (595). Though it is difficult to know how audiences engaged the knowledge they received from the various forms of the lyceum, archival documents show that lyceums did, in fact, encourage, model, and in some cases provide opportunities for critically engaging the information they disseminated. By creating an environment supportive of discussing and exchanging knowledge, the lyceum likely fostered and supported an appreciation for knowledge, learning, deliberation, critical thinking, and inquiry (or, intellectualism).

The speeches of local Ohio lyceum leaders Timothy Walker and Henry Barnes Curtis show that, like Holbrook, they believed lyceums should do more than disseminate knowledge. Walker stated that the knowledge spread by lyceums should not be received passively by the audience but should be under the command of the receiver (8). He argued that lectures provide "the materials for your own minds to act upon: but the benefit will only be completed when you have actually brought your own minds thus to act" (11–12). By the end of his speech, Curtis pushed lyceums to do more than diffuse knowledge:

> It is therefore among the objects of our society, to *rouse* the human mind from its slumberings and indolence, to which like our bodies it is so prone, and awaken in it an energy, that shall enable it to rise, to that rank, to which it so preeminently belongs in the scale of intellect. (6–7)

Like Walker, Curtis believed the lyceum should interest and engage participants' minds, and not just disseminate knowledge to an unthinking audience.

The *Cleveland Herald and Gazette*'s review of a lecture given by Holbrook to youth in Cleveland, Ohio, in October of 1838 indicates Holbrook both educated and inspired his audience in practice (and not just theory):

> [Holbrook] seemed to open to new avenues of knowledge—to give them a clear insight into matters of science—and to unfold to them a new way of improving their own minds of adding to their stock of learning, and of promoting the educational interests of their little friends in different parts of our country and the world.

If this review is an honest and sincere one, we can assume Holbrook treated the lyceum lecture as a tool for stimulating minds rather than as simply a tool for disseminating information to a passive audience.

According to the annals and meeting minutes of four Ohio lyceum associations, lyceum meetings followed the interactive vision Holbrook described in his early writings. These annals and minutes indicate that the purpose of these gatherings was mutual improvement of its members through investigation, discussion, and debate of a variety of issues. For example, the minute book of the Ohio Williams Lyceum Society of Greenfield Academy (1844–46) noted, "The object of this Society shall be the mutual improvement of all its members in the investigation and communication of truth by means of public speaking." The Constitution of the Martinsburg Lyceum of Ohio states, "This society shall be known by the name of the Martinsburg Lyceum, its meetings to be holden weekly, and its exercises to consist chiefly of debates lectures composition and declamation." These minutes make evident that lyceum meetings did indeed consist of speeches followed by debates and sometimes a tallying of votes at the end.

Lyceum periodicals fostered inquiry by asking questions and modeling learning through dialogue. For example, some issues of *Scientific Tracts* contained several questions at the end of the issue to support reflection on the material covered by the journal. The first issue of *Scientific Tracts*, an issue on the atmosphere, included nineteen pages of informational text followed by fifty-six questions that tested the reader's understanding of the material, including questions like, "What vital process in the animal kingdom is conducted by the atmosphere?"; "How many times do persons commonly respire in a minute?"; and "About how much air is received into the lungs at each inhalation?" (20). In the preface to the list of questions, the article states the purpose of the questions is to further engage readers to compensate for the necessarily brief coverage of the subject of the issue. An Ohio lyceum periodical titled *Youth's Lyceum*[10] used its presentation of information to promote active learning. In fact, the first issue of the journal contained a dialogue between mother and son about lyceums, questions and answers about the Earth, a dialogue between two children about going to the lyceum to learn about things, a dialogue between a brother and sister about the arrival of the new *Youth's Lyceum*, a dialogue about what the word *lyceum* means, and a dialogue about geography. In the dialogue on geography, one boy asks another a series of questions about hemispheres, oceans, state capitals, and states, and the other boy answers the questions. By presenting information through dialogue, conversation, and question-and-answer, these journals modeled engagement in the learning process.

In addition to encouraging discussions and debates about the content disseminated, lyceum lectures, meetings, and periodicals also promoted reading, writing, and speaking as activities for disseminating and processing knowledge. For both lyceum lectures and lyceum meetings, speakers wrote, read, and delivered their lectures. Local newspapers also advertised and reported on lectures and meetings and often published excerpts from or the full texts of lectures. Some lectures were also printed by publishers and sold to the public to extend the reach of the lecture. For lyceum periodicals, contributors wrote and the audience read the information being dispersed. *Youth's Lyceum* even invited readers, in its second issue, to contribute: "to be in some degree instrumental in awakening in the minds of those now treading the dangerous paths of youth" (17).

Lyceums also promoted reading as part of the learning process. Holbrook, in the articles of the lyceum constitution, listed books among the things lyceums should obtain ("Associations" 595–96), and he listed the increased need for and popularity of libraries as one of the benefits of lyceums: "The demands immediately and uniformly created for books by the meetings and exercises of lyceums, have led to the enlargement of public libraries, and induced individuals to procure private libraries for their own use" (*American Lyceum* 7).[11] The Martinsburg (Ohio) Lyceum constitution mentions motivating participants to read as one of the benefits of lyceums: "whereas one of the best means of developing the native powers of the mind is by combinations in the form of societies the advantages of which are to cause reading reflection and discrimination." In multiple ways, then, reading, writing, and speaking were central to the intellectual work of lyceums—helping to spread knowledge and stimulate interest in ideas.

In her analysis of the lyceum as a cultural force, Angela G. Ray raises the question of whether or not the lyceum lecture functioned as a "consensus builder," promoting "consent to the norms and values of the professional class of white Protestant New England" (185–88). She claims that while participants took turns speaking on a topic, they didn't actually engage in discussions about the topics (19). While lectures most certainly could have promoted consensus and may not have been followed by discussions in all cases, archival documents show that in practice some organizations did facilitate post-lecture deliberations. In fact, in his study of Ohio lyceum participants' reaction to prominent lecturers from 1850 to 1870, David Mead argued the main responsibility of lecturers was to incite thought and discussion. In doing so, he claims, lyceums "encouraged reading," "promoted community interest in intellectual and moral problems," and "provided pleasure and inspiration for thousands of Western people who were eager for useful, intelligent participation in the progress of America" (23). The lectures could also have inspired participants to seek out more knowledge about subjects. In addition, whether or not the lyceum functioned as a "consensus builder" also would have depended on individual participants. Some may have treated lectures as transmitting knowledge; others may have been moved to think about and discuss or debate topics further. And Ray herself admits that "the structure of the lyceum and the mores that it upheld created space for alternative views and for lecturers who diverged from presumptive ideals" (188).

This examination of lyceum activities suggests several lyceums likely encouraged participants to think about, engage in discussions about, and read, write, and speak about a variety of subjects—and consequently would have made learning collaborative, engaging, and desirable. In conjunction with a reexamination of the useful knowledge disseminated by nineteenth-century lyceums, this research demonstrates lyceums both provided an array of knowledge and created an atmosphere that could have supported the nineteenth-century desire not only to seek knowledge but also to discuss and share it with others—characteristics we should recognize as elements of intellectualism.

TRANSFORMATION OF THE POSTBELLUM LYCEUM

The arrival of the Civil War in 1861 resulted in the relative disappearance of the lyceum. According to one historian, all remaining lectures addressed the war (both in the North and the South) and served more as propaganda than as education or entertainment (Bode 247). To help revive the lyceum after the Civil War, scholar and journalist James Redpath started the first lyceum bureau in 1868.[12] Lyceum bureaus organized and promoted traveling groups that, like the antebellum lyceum, included lectures. These bureaus, however, added to the lyceum stage dramatic and musical performances, mesmerists, phrenologists, and other forms of entertainment. In addition, lecturers at this time became more famous, traveled more, and made more money than they had previously.

This new form of the lyceum experienced great popularity between 1875 and 1900 because of a number of favorable conditions: increased prosperity, the spread of the temperance and women's suffrage movements, the growth of cities, improvement in transportation, and effective advertising by lyceum bureaus (Brigance 122). It was during this period that women became more involved and more prominent on the lyceum platform. While some women participated as entertainers and performers, a number entered as promoters of social reform—seeking both to inform their audience and move them to action.[13]

According to critics, under the control of lyceum bureaus, the postbellum lyceum transformed into a commercial venture focused more on entertaining than instructing the audience. John S. Noffsinger has claimed that under the influence of lyceum bureaus the modern lyceum became a commercial one that—like popular magazines—gave the audience what it wanted (115–18). Carl Bode has said the lyceum after the Civil War was more about entertainment: "Education had pretty well deserted the lecture platform" (248–49). David Mead acknowledged that during the 1860s and after, the "cultural contribution of the Western lyceum" waned when profits and entertainment became the priority (23). Most recently, Angela G. Ray has argued that by the 1870s and 1880s the lyceum was seen as a platform for comics, humorists, singers, and impersonators (5).

Archival documents support critics' accusations that lyceums became more commercial and focused more on entertainment than education after the Civil War. For example, the community annals (1863–83) for Sandy Spring, Maryland, document a change in the community's lyceum. In the entry for 1876–77, the annals stated,

> A proper mixture of instruction and entertainment is what this Lyceum was built for; and if your historian is not mistaken in apprehending that a disproportionate place is being given to the comic and the droll, this is the right time and place to sound the alarm. (169)

An 1895 article in the *New England Magazine* also documents a change in the American lyceum. In this article, nineteenth-century journalist E. P. Powell wrote that the lyceum had become more about money and entertainment in its later years. He described the 1890s lyceum as follows: "The lyceum as it exists to-day is a starring exhibition approaching very nearly to theatricals." He also said that the costs rose and only the biggest cities could secure the most popular speakers (736).

Promotional materials for lyceum performers in the late nineteenth and early twentieth centuries also confirm the emphasis on and addition of entertaining performances. An 1890s flier for Dr. Georgia Merriman's lectures on food analysis[14] promotes "her ability to interest and instruct an audience" and describes her lectures as an "instructive and attractive evening's entertainment." Comments on promotional fliers for Ohio native Viola D. Romans[15] that appeared in the early 1900s included "While she instructs as well as entertains, her manner and diction hold attention from the first," and "[Romans] is able to present her thoughts in such a way as to command the interest and enthusiasm of any intelligent audience." One late nineteenth-century flier for "The Lyceum Entertainers" contained pictures of the women performers and described the program they provide as follows: "These young ladies give a program of excellent music, some serious readings, and a proper part of delightful entertainment."

Despite the changes in the lyceum late in the nineteenth century recorded in both contemporary and nineteenth-century sources, the lyceum continued to include lectures that informed and engaged audiences. In fact, after the Civil War, the lyceum opened its stage to a greater variety of speakers[16] (including white and black women and black men) who used the lyceum stage as a platform for political and social reform. Some of these speakers, like Elizabeth Cady Stanton,[17] made their cases for reform through the use of "entertaining anecdotes and stories" (Hogan and Hogan 426). Others' speeches, like those of Frederick Douglass, were "unabashedly political and partisan" (Ray 137). In fact, communications professor William N. Brigance has argued that despite its transition into a more commercial business and its eventual decline, the lyceum from 1865 to 1930 served an important function in the postbellum United States: "From it came the main stimulus to American adult education, reading courses, book clubs, correspondence schools, the immense business-book publishing business. It has been the firing line of our anti-slavery, temperance, woman's rights, and anti-narcotics crusades" (129).

Similarly, Joseph Kett describes the lyceum in the 1870s and 1880s as "increasingly eclectic," and he explains the changes as the result of greater competition with new amusements. The response, he claims, was to diversify lyceums. Contrary to other critics, Kett argues this diversification "did not put an end to serious lecturing." It did, however, open the lyceum to criticisms and led to its no longer being viewed as a significant disseminator of "popular education" (147–48). In other words, though they had to share the stage with jugglers, musicians, comedians, and actors, many post–Civil War lyceum speakers informed, entertained, and intellectually stimulated their audiences. As Ray has described it, among the results of the transformation of the content and form of the lyceum was a transformation in the role of the audience: from "participants and learners" to "spectators and judges" or potential "social reformers" (177). While the role of "spectators and judges" was likely passive, the role of potential "social reformers" would not have been.

It is worth noting that though the inclusion of musical, dramatic, and comedic performances was new to the lyceum stage after the Civil War, from the beginning the lyceum sought to both entertain and educate its audience. In an 1829 promotional leaflet entitled *American Lyceum, or Society for the Improvement of Schools and Diffusion of Useful Knowledge,*[18] Josiah Holbrook lists as one of the advantages of existing lyceums the production of education and entertainment at a relatively low cost (5–10). The Sandy Spring annals referred to earlier also mentioned that the lyceum was designed to provide a "proper mixture of instruction and entertainment" (169). According to Scott, the performance aspect to lectures was important even before the war. "By the late 1840s, a public lecture was expected to entertain as well as instruct and inspire, and the newspaper reviews always assessed the quality of the performance as well as the substance of the message" (805).

In her work on the history of the American lyceum, Ray described the lyceum's blending of entertainment and instruction as a complicated one from the beginning, with entertainment present in early lyceums and an emphasis on learning present in the later lyceums (3–6). In fact, she said, "The word lyceum embodied the paradoxes of playful learning and serious fun" (6). Recognizing the lyceum's life-long effort to instruct and entertain, it seems that critics (past and present) were troubled by the inclusion of and emphasis on performances designed solely for entertainment and not by lectures that both instructed and entertained the audience. In light of the late nineteenth-century development of a cultural hierarchy that ranked some art and entertainment highbrow and some lowbrow (Levine, *Highbrow/Lowbrow*), it is also possible that criticism followed the inclusion of entertainment considered lowbrow, like juggling, acting, impersonations, and performances by those rhetoric scholar Frederick Antezak has described as "'table-thumping' spiritualists, 'hack' politicians, phrenologists, and 'buffoon-style comedians'" (73–74).

For some critics (then and now), the transformation of the lyceum into a more commercial and entertainment-driven venue was a symbol of the "intellectual deterioration" of the American public. Noted previously in my review of contemporary calls of crisis and decline in American literacy and learning, this tendency to believe American society has slipped from a previous intellectual golden age to an era of intellectual apathy persists, perpetuated by limited notions of intellectualism. It is possible, however, that Americans' nineteenth-century intellectual interests in the lyceum were redirected to other activities and institutions, such as the Chautauqua,[19] and later to other institutions like twentieth-century labor colleges (discussed in chapter 3).

My reexamination of what has been called the postbellum transformation of the American lyceum suggests that though more forms of entertainment were included on the lyceum stage, so too were some of the most influential lectures of the nineteenth century. In addition, while the change in investment on the part of lyceum organizers from making knowledge accessible to the public to making a profit affected the reputation of lyceums and the message they were sending about knowledge, the lyceum continued to inform its audience and foster interest in and engagement with ideas—characteristics of the view of intellectualism this book argues for.

ACCESS AND AUDIENCE

Because I argue that the lyceum fostered intellectualism by providing access to information and opportunities to engage ideas critically, I end my analysis of lyceums with an examination of the factors that influenced access to the lyceum and the ways in which it made information accessible to its audience. As stated earlier, I chose the American lyceum as one of my

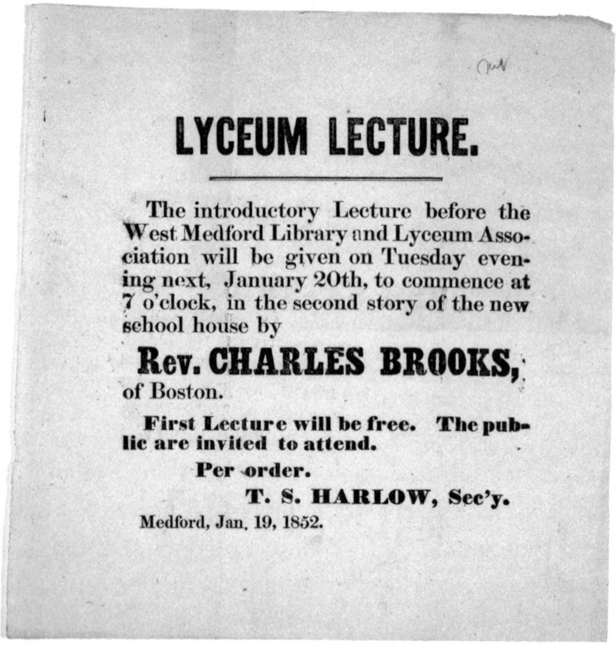
LYCEUM LECTURE.

The introductory Lecture before the West Medford Library and Lyceum Association will be given on Tuesday evening next, January 20th, to commence at 7 o'clock, in the second story of the new school house by

Rev. CHARLES BROOKS,
of Boston.

First Lecture will be free. The public are invited to attend.

Per order.
T. S. HARLOW, Sec'y.
Medford, Jan. 19, 1852.

Announcement for a Medford, Massachusetts, lyceum lecture. Printed Ephemera Collection; Portfolio 61, Folder 1. The Library of Congress American Memory website.

sites of investigation because it made knowledge accessible to many in the nineteenth century who may not have had the time, money, or ability to access education in other forms. Though it is difficult to know precisely how many people attended, some estimates claim about four hundred thousand people a week attended public lectures in the North and West by the 1850s (Scott 800). And, at its peak the lyceum was said to have been attended by approximately 5 million people a year between 1875 and 1900 (Brigance 122).

Josiah Holbrook's 1826 article and 1829 leaflet contain specific reference to his desire for lyceums to be widely accessible. For example, one of the articles Holbrook proposed for lyceum constitutions read, "Any person may be a member of the society, by paying to the Treasurer, annually, one dollar. And ten dollars paid at any one time, will constitute a person a member for life" ("Associations" 595). In addition, one of the duties he lists for state lyceum boards is "to diffuse the greatest quantity of useful information among the various classes of the community" (596).[20] The nineteenth-century announcements for lyceum meetings and lectures I located in my archival research support the argument that the lyceum invited a general public to attend lectures and meetings. Here are two examples of such announcements.

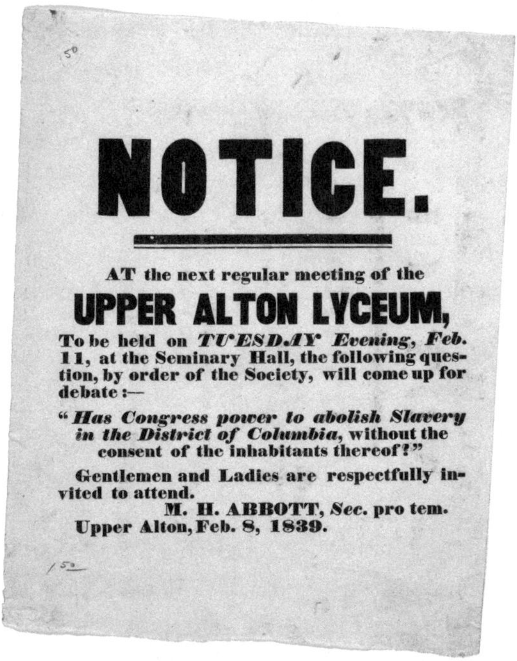
NOTICE.

AT the next regular meeting of the

UPPER ALTON LYCEUM,

To be held on *TUESDAY Evening, Feb.* 11, at the Seminary Hall, the following question, by order of the Society, will come up for debate :—

"*Has Congress power to abolish Slavery in the District of Columbia*, without the consent of the inhabitants thereof?"

Gentlemen and Ladies are respectfully invited to attend.

M. H. ABBOTT, *Sec.* pro tem.

Upper Alton, Feb. 8, 1839.

Announcement for a meeting of the Upper Alton Lyceum in Illinois. Printed Ephemera Collection; Portfolio 15, Folder 15. The Library of Congress American Memory website.

Lyceum periodicals also claimed wide access as a goal for their dissemination of useful knowledge. In the first issue of *Scientific Tracts,* the prefatory material stated the information was "intended to be brought within the comprehension, and to meet the wants of the great mass of the community; especially of the industrious classes, who have neither time nor opportunities to devote their lives to intellectual pursuits." *Family Lyceum,* in its first issue, similarly claimed a broad target audience: "For parents and children, teachers and the taught, business man and man of leisure, to students and mechanic, philosopher and farmer, both sexes, all classes, all ages" (1).

Despite these declarations of wide accessibility for the American lyceum, most evidence shows that, in practice, access was sometimes limited, often dictated by cost, gender, race, and affiliation. First, the cost of attending lyceum lectures or participating in town lyceum organizations would have prevented access for some. For example, the fees were comparatively low for the wealthy, merchants, and skilled workers, but would most likely have been too much for the poorest of the community. Also, though the cost was quite low at first, it increased over the years. In fact, by 1828 Holbrook suggested charging two dollars for a one-year membership and twenty dollars for a lifetime membership—doubling the cost from two years before (Ray 22–24).

In addition to cost, participation in lyceum organizations sometimes depended upon an invitation or a membership in a religious or other organization. For instance, according to meeting minutes, participation in the Allen Missionary Lyceum was based on religious affiliation and student status at Ohio Wesleyan University. The Williams Lyceum was open only to students at the academy, and participants had to take part in the regular exercises at least once every two weeks to maintain their membership. Members of the Martinsburg Lyceum had to be voted in by two-thirds of the existing members, pay twenty-five cents, and sign a constitution. These restrictions on participation meant that not all persons could participate in the discussions and debates—or in the cultivation of intellectualism—taking place at these meetings.

Gender and race were also factors that influenced access to lyceums. Though the nineteenth-century meeting minutes, announcements, and promotional material I accessed did not provide evidence that people were explicitly excluded from lyceums based on gender or race, I did find evidence that, as Ray and Scott have argued, white males were most likely the typical audience in the early years of the lyceum, especially at local lyceum meetings. For example, in his 1829 leaflet advertising lyceums, Holbrook mentions women meeting separately from men: "Females have conducted a course of mutual exercises among themselves, by spending together, during the summer, one afternoon in a week for reading, composition, and improvement in the various branches of an accomplished and enlightened education." In addition, while an 1841 newspaper report about the Cleveland Lyceum in the *Cleveland Herald* mentioned the attendance of women, it stated, "Our young men will find this Society worthy of their attention." I also located a list of participants in the meeting minutes for the Williams Lyceum that appears to contain only male names. Finally, my review of the *Cleveland Herald* archives revealed the development of a separate colored men's lyceum in Cleveland in 1842.

While this handful of references to race and gender does not conclusively demonstrate the inclusion or exclusion of lyceum participants based on these characteristics, it is consistent with historians' assessments of the lyceum audience. Ray has argued that though public lectures included a more wide-ranging audience, the members of town or village lyceum organizations were primarily "elite or upwardly mobile men in the community" (25). According to Donald Scott, while audiences for the public lyceum did vary by age and occupation (including men and women from their mid-teens to early sixties working as artisans, mechanics, farmers, lawyers, teachers, professors, doctors, clergymen, shopkeepers, merchants), the primary audience for the lectures was "almost exclusively a northern public," composed of what could be called the middle class and overwhelmingly white Anglo-Saxon Protestants (800–809). He described attendees as "aspiring and ambitious," saying, "The lecture-going public was thus made up of people who perceived themselves in motion, in a state of preparation or expectation" (801).

David Mead described the audience for Ohio lyceum lectures as "composed of a few intellectuals and a large body of plain citizens—farmers, mechanics, and shopkeepers to whom 'culture' meant useful knowledge and practical, provocative ideas." He has also described audiences as including rich and poor, educated and uneducated. He claims, in fact, Western lyceum audiences differed from those in the East.

> Westerners were a practical, mercantile people who stoutly resisted the efforts of learned lecturers to instill in them a taste for philosophy. . . . Western listeners were critical and independent, and, if a lecture was dull or otherwise unpleasing, they were not averse to stamping out of the lecture hall. (20–22)

According to these scholars, though not accessible to all, lyceums were attended by a fairly wide range of people.

In some cases, opportunities for participation in lyceums—both as audience members and lyceum speakers—increased after the Civil War. While women did participate in knowledge societies before the Civil War, they had more opportunities for participating in and even speaking before lyceum organizations after the war. And, as noted earlier, several notable women and African Americans began speaking on the lyceum stage after the Civil War.

Once again, it is important to recognize that because access to lyceums was, for some, limited based on cost and social and cultural affiliations, the lyceum on some level perpetuated the traditional notion that intellectuals are prominent white males in the middle and upper classes. Despite these limitations, the lyceum's primary mission was to make useful knowledge accessible to participants. In this way, the lyceum did increase access to knowledge—and to opportunities for engaging with ideas.

Access to the lyceum was one issue. Another was efforts made to make the knowledge being disseminated accessible to the audience. In his 1829 leaflet Holbrook said, "The instruction given by lectures or dissertations, like that in a more mutual form, is intended to be of a familiar and practical character, that it may be brought within the comprehension of the most untutored mind" (*American Lyceum* 4). Lyceum lectures made education accessible to those who had less schooling or lacked access to reading materials or formal education because they presented information in an oral and sometimes visual form. Significantly, then, as long as people could afford the entrance fee or organization dues, lyceum lectures opened to them the knowledge and messages about education contained in the speeches. Similarly, participation in local lyceum discussions and debates would also have been accessible to those with little schooling.

Holbrook's goal of making the knowledge spread by lyceums accessible is evident in his lyceum periodicals. In the first issue of *Scientific Tracts*, the editor's remarks state explicitly that the journal will "present things, properties, principles, applications, in the simplicity of nature, and not through labyrinths of terms, and mazes of declarations" (23). In a later issue on entomology the author wrote that his article was "prepared for the *general reader*" (184). In *Youth's Lyceum* the editors speak directly to children as the target audience, stating, "We intend to have the articles on the sciences as plain and easy to be understood as we can make them, and we hope you will not read them hastily and without understanding" (vol. 1, no. 1). Making information accessible in this way increased the influence lyceums could have on the nineteenth-century public—especially the public that had less schooling or little access to information in other forms.

Though the nineteenth-century American lyceum was not always accessible to all Americans, the lyceum did open access to knowledge to many who may not have otherwise had access. In addition, the lyceum also made knowledge accessible by presenting information orally, visually, and at a level designed to be understood by "an untutored mind." While critics may argue that making knowledge accessible to wide audiences means "dumbing it down" or reducing its intellectual content, my examination of the nineteenth-century lyceum (its content, activities, and transformation) weighs heavily against such an argument.

The American lyceum dissolved in the early 1900s, giving way to other forms of adult education (including early twentieth-century labor colleges, the focus of chapter 3). My reevaluation of this significant site of literacy and learning in the nineteenth century helps demonstrate how a revised view of intellectualism not based on a dichotomous or hierarchical view of learning and education, but rather focused on an interest in, appreciation for, and engagement with knowledge, deliberation, debate, critical thinking, and inquiry can help us recognize and even celebrate the intellectual work of the lyceum.

My review of lyceum archives in conjunction with existing scholarship on the lyceum makes clear that the lyceum sent the message that knowledge and education are valuable, that it made a wide array of knowledge accessible to participants, and that it encouraged and provided opportunities for participants to develop their minds. Even the transformation of the lyceum to a stage including many forms of entertainment—the characteristic of the lyceum scholars have most consistently criticized—did not end the lyceum's dissemination of knowledge nor its ability to incite an interest in learning. These characteristics, I argue, make the lyceum a significant site of American intellectualism in the nineteenth century.

One of the most important implications of my reevaluation of the American lyceum is its refutation of the longstanding cultural belief that the pursuit of useful knowledge for a practical purpose is not intellectual. In fact, I argue that my research demonstrates that in their dissemination of useful knowledge lyceums promoted and likely fostered intellectualism. Because this criterion is one of the main reasons why many sites of learning (including the lyceum, labor colleges, and adult GED writing workshops) are relegated nonintellectual, contesting it can have a significant effect on Americans' views and valuing of the education that takes place at nonelite institutions. My analysis of the labor colleges in the next chapter furthers this discussion and ties it to workers' education in the twentieth century.

chapter three

INTELLECTUALISM AND EDUCATION FOR A PRACTICAL PURPOSE

The Twentieth-Century Labor College

IN THE WAKE OF THE lyceum movement and in the midst of the American workers' education and labor movements, labor colleges were established in the United States early in the twentieth century. Founded and supported by workers, labor leaders, and labor sympathizers, labor colleges were full-time, one- to three-year schools designed (1) to educate adult workers about the social, cultural, political, and economic factors affecting labor, and (2) to train them to be successful labor movement leaders and activists. To accomplish this, labor colleges implemented a curriculum with a balance of "informational" courses on subjects like labor history, economics, law, foreign labor, and modern industry, and "tool" courses teaching workers skills such as report writing, journalism, public speaking, organizing methods, and drama. The mission of labor colleges was, in fact, "NOT to educate workers out of their class," but to provide workers with the knowledge and tools to help enact social change, specifically to create a reconstructed social order under the control of workers (*Report to the Second International Conference* 8).

Like the lyceum, labor colleges have been overlooked as sponsors of intellectualism in U.S. history; in this case it is because their focus on activism is associated with learning for a "practical" purpose, and because they have been criticized for promoting doctrinaire thinking about issues relevant to the labor movement. In addition, working people have often been portrayed as "accommodating or acquiescent" (Altenbaugh, *Education* 11), qualities considered non- or anti-intellectual. Inherent in these criticisms are a series of misguided assumptions, including the following: education for a "practical" purpose cannot foster intellectualism, the dissemination of ideological information interferes with a person's ability to think critically about that information, labor colleges did not teach or support critical thinking, and students did not enter the programs prepared to be analytical, independent thinkers. If we accept these assumptions, then we fail to recognize the broad range of intellectual activities found and nurtured at U.S. labor colleges, and we overlook the value of the education and experience students received there—reinforcing contemporary restrictive beliefs about intellectualism that, among other things, continue to devalue the work of today's laborers and unions.

While the contributions of U.S. labor colleges to the twentieth-century educational landscape have been well documented (Altenbaugh, Howlett, Kates, Kett, Carlson, Clark, Smith, Wan), this chapter goes beyond existing research to examine, more specifically, the labor college's contributions to twentieth-century intellectualism. In order to better understand the contributions labor colleges made to the public's intellectual development in the twentieth century, this chapter draws on archival documents from Brookwood Labor College (founded in 1921 in Katonah, New York), the most popular and widely recognized labor college in the United States. In their documentation of Brookwood's purpose, institutional structure and organization, curriculum, teaching and learning practices, students' attitudes and motivations, and the access to education the school provided to workers, these archives demonstrate how American labor colleges like Brookwood used activist educational practices to inspire workers to be active, analytical learners and motivate them to educate others through their activist work. With the broadened view of intellectualism I am putting forth in this book—one that values the intellectual import of the desire to learn and the work of engaging in the practice and process of inquiry, understanding, and critical thinking—the public (and particularly critics who today view labor unions as anti-intellectual) can recognize twentieth-century labor colleges like Brookwood as educational spaces that provided an intellectual core for laborers and the labor movement.

LABOR COLLEGES AND WORKERS' EDUCATION

The work of historians Richard Altenbaugh, Charles F. Howlett, and Joseph Kett documents well the educational, social, and cultural contributions of twentieth-century labor colleges, and Brookwood Labor College in particular. According to them, labor colleges were a response to what American laborers felt was a harmful public education system and an ineffective labor organization, the American Federation of Labor (AFL). Critics have noted the AFL (formed in 1886) did not work for broad social reform or serve workers but rather aligned itself with business groups, endorsing public education and voting as the appropriate means to liberate the American worker intellectually and politically (Kett 352).[1] For many workers, however, public education was inadequate, unfair, and sometimes inaccessible.[2] Workers felt public schools deceived them in an effort to "keep them docile and submissive" and reinforce the existing social system. In 1896, Eugene V. Debs[3] called the formal educational system in the United States at best "not equipped to solve labor problems," and at worst "arrogantly hostile to labor" (ctd. in Altenbaugh *Education* 20–22). James H. Maurer, president of the Brookwood Labor College board of directors, described the public schools this way:

> The individuality of the student is suppressed. The attempt is made to mold all minds by the same pattern and independence, originality, and self-reliance are discouraged. Our children are being trained like dogs and ponies, not developed as individuals. Such methods, together with the vicious propaganda on social and economic questions to which the children are subjected, produce just the results that the conservative and reactionary elements of the country want, namely, uniformity of thought and conduct, no originality or self-reliance except for money-making schemes, a worshipful attitude toward those who have wealth and power, intolerance for anything that the business element condemns, and ignorance of the great social and economic forces that are shaping the destinies of all of us. (Workers' Education Bureau 11)

For Maurer and other laborers and labor leaders, to overcome such circumstances and effect social change, they had to educate themselves. Workers' education programs designed to foster awareness, critical thinking, and independence were developed and became widespread as a result.[4]

Workers' education programs existed in a variety of forms, including union-sponsored, university-sponsored, and independent programs.[5] According to Altenbaugh's history, though early union-sponsored workers' education strove for social reform, by the mid-1930s its objectives had become mostly utilitarian, focused on training union bureaucrats who would perform the desires of the union without question.[6] Cooptation of these programs by the AFL, declining trade union membership, and internal political disputes contributed to this problem. University or college-sponsored workers' education programs, on the other hand, tended to emphasize the individual's growth rather than social-class consciousness. The challenge for school-sponsored programs was that they were bound by the philosophies and policies of the institution, much of which was influenced by industry and business.[7] Consequently, labor groups were skeptical of university-sponsored programs[8] and workers were not given much power in the development of the programs. In Altenbaugh's opinion, "In the end, institutions of higher education, despite their self-proclaimed liberalism, did not create an environment of intellectual and political freedom for working-class students" (*Education* 44–54).

In contrast to union and university-sponsored programs, American labor colleges were independent workers' education programs, funded through individual donations and trade-union scholarships. Because of their independence, they had more political autonomy and the freedom to enact a more radical curriculum and innovative pedagogical practices. Not bound by the philosophy or policies of unions, business, or universities, labor colleges endeavored to empower workers by educating them in theory and in practice about social change, economics, politics, and other social issues related to labor. Their commitment to social change is what distinguished them most from union- and university-sponsored workers' education.

While many labor colleges were started in the early twentieth century, Brookwood Labor College attracted the most students, helped set the tone for workers' education, and graduated more well-known labor leaders than any other labor college[9] (Kates 76). Historian Joseph Kett has referred to Brookwood as "the only postwar labor college unaffiliated with a union, college, or university" (360).[10] Its independent status made it, in the words of the school's 1936 director, "an institutional orphan, fathered by no particular faction, right or left" (Smith 7). The vice president of Brookwood, Fannia M. Cohn, wrote that the "non-factional" policy of Brookwood made it appealing to the whole labor movement (10). For these reasons, archival documents from the school, including course syllabi and materials, student writings, institution publications, promotional materials, reports, memos, and correspondence,[11] can reveal labor colleges' potential for intellectual activity and what forms of intellectualism were practiced and cultivated there.

BROOKWOOD'S PURPOSE

In March 1921, labor leaders, union radicals, socialist leaders, and educators met in New York City for the first national conference on workers' education. The result of the meeting was the opening of Brookwood Labor College later that year.[12] The design of Brookwood was based on the following plan drawn up by conference participants and published in an April 1, 1921, *New York Times* article titled "Plan Workers' College":

> First—That a new social order is needed and is coming—in fact, that is already on the way.
>
> Second—That education will not only hasten its coming, but will reduce to a minimum and perhaps do away entirely with a resort to violent methods.
>
> Third—That the workers are the ones who will usher in the new social order.
>
> Fourth—That there is immediate need for a workers' college with a broad curriculum, located amid healthy country surroundings, where the students can completely apply themselves to the task at hand. (8)

The purpose of Brookwood, as articulated in this public plan, was to educate workers so they could aid the labor movement in establishing a new social order. A passage from Brookwood's student application form describes the purpose of the school similarly:

> In determining on courses, teaching methods, and all matters of educational policy, Brookwood asks one question: What can a resident school do to enable American workers to work more effectively in the American labor movement? . . . Brookwood is interested in the ultimate and spiritual aims of the labor movement, as well as in its immediate, material aims. . . . Finally, Brookwood is an integral part of the American labor movement and exists only to serve it. Its graduates go back to mine, mill and shop, and to their unions, not to get something out of the movement, but to put something into it, not to get jobs but to do work. This spirit of complete, practical devotion to the movement is the spirit of Brookwood. (*Questionnaire*)

In other words, students were expected to use their training at Brookwood to address labor problems, not (like lyceum participants) for the goal of individual social mobility or personal advancement.

In her explanation for why students came to the school, labor journalism teacher Helen Norton said students came for knowledge "about their own unions, about the history of the labor movement in this and other countries" and training in how to use that knowledge "to express their ideals so the crowd will get them and be moved to *action* by them." Sarah Cleghorn (one of the earliest teachers at Brookwood) said the students had a "single-minded" purpose: "They wanted literary feeling, personal expression, not for life in general, but for the labor movement alone"[13] (ctd. in Altenbaugh, *Education* 93; 137). Stated another way in the December 1, 1923, issue of the *Brookwood Review* (the school newspaper), education at Brookwood was described as *not* being "education just for education's sake, leading nowhere save to individual advancement" (1); education at Brookwood was education for activism.

Some critics, including historian Richard Hofstadter, would dismiss the intellectual import of labor colleges at this point, arguing intellectualism is education for education's sake, not for the sake of a social movement or a practical purpose. However, I argue that Brookwood's goal of serving the labor movement did not result in the absence or stifling of intellectualism because (as archival documents demonstrate) the students' motivation, the institutional structure and organization, the curriculum, the pedagogical practices, and the activism at Brookwood all promoted and supported the desire to learn, deliberate, and critically engage with ideas.

BROOKWOOD STUDENTS

While other scholars have looked to Brookwood's teaching and promotional materials to assess the school's contributions to twentieth-century education, little attention has been paid to the students' own writings and what they can tell us about their attitudes, interests, and contributions. An important resource for this data is the autobiographical essays students wrote when they started the program. In these essays, students summarized their past experiences and articulated their interest in attending the school. These autobiographies show students entered the program for the same reason the institution existed: service to the labor movement. They also show that students came to Brookwood with significant experience as workers, union members, and members of political organizations. Based on students' comments, these experiences and their interests in political and social issues fueled their interest in their education and motivated them to engage in the learning and thinking practices that were part of the Brookwood experience. Students' attitudes toward learning, then, would have helped Brookwood foster intellectualism among participants.

In her autobiography, Rhoda Pearson[14] of New Hampshire wrote that she was interested in the "radical movement" and had been the head of a Progressive Club before entering Brookwood. To Pearson, Brookwood was an opportunity to learn how to help build a classless society. She wrote, also, of her genuine interest in learning:

> All through high school and college I had taken courses purely from my interest in them and not from a desire to pick a vocation or trade, feeling (perhaps as all young people feel) that there was some big thing that I wanted to have a hand in some day if I could only keep following my interests long enough.

Another student, George Nordstrom, went to high school in Wisconsin, had some vocational training, joined the Wisconsin Socialist Party, and was a leader in fighting against poor working conditions. He wrote, "That's why I'm here heart and soul in the work, hopeful that my six months here will give me the necessary knowledge to become most effective in the movement." Similarly, Alvom Rosenfield wrote in his autobiographical essay, titled "Success Story," that he came to Brookwood to prepare to play a part in the struggle to "overthrow the system."

Paul W. Fehnel from Pennsylvania, the son of working-class parents, left school at age fifteen to apprentice as a printer. He was a member of the Young People's Socialist League and the Unemployed Citizens' League. In his essay he confessed, "I feel that I made some mistakes in the past, so here I am at Brookwood to learn more about the labor movement, tactics to pursue, etc. that I may avoid the pitfalls in future organizing work." Also motivated by an interest in becoming an effective labor leader, an unnamed woman from a farm in Indiana who had worked in a hosiery mill and had previously attended the summer school for workers in Madison, Wisconsin, wrote, "At present I'm very interested in learning enough about the labor problems to become an organizer or to help teach in workers' schools. I feel it is my duty to go out and help workers with their problems."

A student named Ben who had not been a laborer but who was seeking such work and an atmosphere for studying, wrote,

> So finally I am here to study and work hard and to conduct some sort of activity. . . . and to meet with and grapple with the problem

> of understanding the ways and thinkings of the American workers and farmers . . .

He also stated, "I was very much impressed and feel that at Brookwood I could study diligently in an atmosphere well suited and most conducive to studying. . . ." And John Strobel wrote that attending Brookwood was a long-time goal. Upon entering the program, he wrote, "I intend to do my best and I am sure that the results will bear out the reputation that Brookwood has established."

In addition to sharing their work experiences and reasons for coming to Brookwood, two students reflected in their essays on the quality of education they received prior to attending. Sophie R. Dornbusch wrote in 1934, "I went through the local grammar and high schools, and received the most biased, prejudiced, and conservative anti-everything ground work of education that could possibly have been anyone's misfortune." Similarly, an unidentified student wrote, "I was disgusted with the mid-class teaching and atmosphere of the college I attended. Now I am happy to be with my own class of people again." Such comments reveal students' awareness of the importance of education and their desire for an education relevant and applicable to their own interests and experiences.

Other selections of student writing further our understanding of students' attitudes toward and interest in learning at Brookwood. A 1923 issue of the *Brookwood Review* stated, "It is inspiring to observe a group of workers assembled from all parts of the United States and some parts of Europe, eager to absorb every bit of knowledge that is offered to them." Nine years later, an article in the *Review* declared, "In place of grades, examinations, and diplomas as incentives to study, Brookwooders have an interest and devotion to labor, which immensely simplifies the teaching problem here." In addition, after visiting Brookwood, President Farrell of the Kansas State College of Agriculture and Applied Science claimed that "[Brookwood] contains only people who are eager to learn. . . . The little group of students at Brookwood exhibit the eager desire to learn that would be a dominant feature of an ideal college . . ." (ctd. in Clark 402).

The above comments, and students' own comments in particular, show students at Brookwood came of their own accord, and they came ready and willing to learn. The interest in learning students brought with them helped create an intellectual environment at Brookwood. And, while their previous work experiences and participation in social and political organizations would have influenced greatly the opinions about politics, economics, and labor they brought with them, Brookwood's program was designed to expand their understanding of these issues and provide the opportunity to think critically about them.

BROOKWOOD'S INSTITUTIONAL ORGANIZATION AND STRUCTURE

Brookwood institutional reports and memos paint a picture of an educational institution designed to eliminate traditional authoritarian relationships between students and teachers and provide students multiple opportunities to participate in the organization and operation of the school. These characteristics of the school supported student learning and critical thinking and would likely have fostered students' intellectual development.

According to school documents, students held positions on every governing body of the institution[15] and they had their own committees to deal with student problems and arrange social functions. They organized their own activities outside the classroom hours and "exercise[d] advisory powers in educational matters" (*Brookwood Bulletin* 15). They were also involved in the hiring and firing of teachers (Altenbaugh, *Education* 157–58). Even outside their service on governing bodies, students and teachers were treated as equals. Students were encouraged to call teachers by their first names, teachers and students participated in extracurricular activities together, and they shared equally in the manual work (including construction, farming, cooking, and maintenance) required for Brookwood to run (Altenbaugh, *Education* 131–32). By creating a more equal relationship between students and teachers, Brookwood avoided imposing educational hierarchies that could have stifled students' intellectual development.

A document titled *Agenda for Student-Faculty Review of the Year's Life and Work at Brookwood* confirms the school's (and teachers') interest in student involvement in curriculum and pedagogy. The agenda contained a list of questions for students, including the following: "Is Brookwood offering the right courses of study?"; "Are there specific suggestions as to teaching methods in any of the courses?"; "Is there too much or too little written work?"; "Is there too much or too little participation in outside activities?"; "How can we have a more cooperative and harmonious community at Brookwood—among students, faculty and staff?"; and "Did we have the right kind and number of outside speakers this year?" The document ends with a statement telling students to "come prepared to express your ideas freely and frankly." As this document shows, Brookwood faculty solicited students' honest opinions, and consequently encouraged students to participate in the design and execution of their education and not just the acquisition of it (as most schools do). Brookwood faculty sought student feedback because they shared with students experience as laborers and a dedication to the labor movement.

Several Brookwood documents illustrate students did, in fact, exercise the power and freedom that the faculty and administration are said to have given them. One example comes from a 1931–32 memorandum students wrote claiming that they were dissatisfied with the opportunities they were being given in some classes to express their opinions:

> It is our opinion that Brookwood classes should be a place in which the students, and not the teachers, do the greater part of the talking. When facts are necessary, however, of course, the teacher must present them. We have felt that in some courses, however, such as the class in Marx, not enough opportunity is given for the ecpression [*sic*] of student thought. Instructors sometimes use class time for the purpose of clarifying their own individual point of view. (Kuhlman and Pierce)

While these comments show that instructors did not always provide students the opportunity to express their ideas, they also demonstrate students spoke up when they wanted change, they valued their own opinions, and they demanded they be able to express them.

Students also critiqued their own performance and participation in the program. In a report to faculty and administrators, students wrote that

> during the year there has developed a general laxness among the student body as a whole, particularly in regard to studies. . . . We believe that to a degree this relaxation is valuable and necessary, but also that much time has been wasted.

The solutions students offered included more faculty control, more effective student organization, and student self-discipline (Kuhlman and Pierce). In another instance, when concerned teachers and administrators told a student he must leave Brookwood because his English-language skills were so poor they impeded his participation in coursework, students responded with a petition. Students wrote to teachers and administrators in defense of the student, Bill Barash, saying, "Whereas Bill Barash has not mustered the mechanics of writing and reading, he has a keen intellect, independence, and originality in thinking, and reads with understanding." The students offered to tutor Barash so he could stay at Brookwood, and the faculty replied by allowing Barash to continue (*Student Petition*).

Brookwood reports and memos also show evidence that students didn't always think alike in their critiques and comments on the administration of Brookwood. A series of documents titled "Statement of the Minority of the Students to the Board of Directors" and "Statement of the Majority of the Students to the Board of Directors" show how students expressed their opinions in smaller groups if they didn't all agree.

As these archival documents indicate, Brookwood was designed to encourage the expression of ideas even if they were contrary to teachers' or others' ideas. They also show that students were invested in their education, exhibited independent thought, and had ample opportunity to shape the program. The fact that students' voices were solicited, heard, and respected outside the classroom (and not just inside it, as I address later) sent students the message that their ideas and opinions were valuable—contributing to Brookwood's ability to create an environment conducive to the practice and cultivation of intellectualism.

THE BROOKWOOD CURRICULUM

Like the knowledge disseminated by lyceums, the Brookwood curriculum has not been recognized as intellectual because it was intended to be "useful" and "practical" in students' lives as workers and because it was viewed by some as doctrinaire or ideological. Curriculum documents from Brookwood show, however, that the foundational understanding of labor issues this curriculum provided empowered students to think through social, political, and economic issues surrounding American labor, to understand their personal experiences in a larger context, and to become more confident leaders and communicators. These skills would have influenced students' participation in intellectual activities and their investment in learning.

In the 1924 *Report to the Second International Conference on Workers' Education*, administrators noted that in order to achieve their purpose of preparing men and women for leadership in the labor movement, students first needed "a point of view" and a "method of approach to their problems," including the ability to find information, interpret the information, and problem-solve based on that information (7). In other words, students could not serve the larger purpose without the skills that encourage them to be critical thinkers and activists. The curriculum was designed, then, to prepare students for such work.

As stated in a 1925 pamphlet advertising the school, "informational" courses were typically taken in the first year of the two-year program and were designed "to train the minds of the students as instruments for acquiring knowledge and thinking through problems, and to lay sound foundations in the study of the social sciences." Courses in this category included economics, advanced economics, American history, history of the American Labor Movement, foreign labor history, history of civilization, trade union organization work, modern industry, labor organization problems, and current events (*Brookwood Labor College*). Susan Kates has described the goal of these courses as helping workers "understand how history, economics, literature, and language in the public system of education perpetuated the status quo in the United States and resulted in the exploitation of the American worker" (76). In trade union organization work, students studied the labor movement alongside issues like political action, economic strikes, collective bargaining, and employers' associations. In addition, with the objective of exposing students to an alternative social system, advanced economics provided a Marxist interpretation of contemporary history and compared American capitalist society with Soviet society (Altenbaugh, *Education* 95). In American history, students learned about "the main forces operating in American life in the past and today, and the role the United States is playing in the modern world." To help them understand the American experience in a larger context, they also read and talked about economic development in other nations (*Brookwood Bulletin* 7).

A closer look at the readings assigned for such courses demonstrates that the emphasis was on giving students a breadth of information at an introductory level that would inform and shape their engagement with the labor movement. Reviews of the texts from academic journals reveal they were texts noticed by scholars and were often intended for college courses. According to a document titled "Books Used in Courses at Brookwood Labor College," five texts were assigned for the first-year course on social economics. *American Economic Life* was a book published in 1925 by Rexford Guy Tugwell, Thomas Munro, and Roy E. Stryker. In a review in *Economic Geography*, it was called successful as an introductory college textbook:

> It is not too elementary for the intelligent college student, and is very much more thorough than certain other works of the type which have recently appeared . . . and will be useful in bringing in an interesting manner to the attention of the young student a knowledge of modern conditions and problems which will stimulate his interest in the principles of the economic sciences, and prepare him for understanding and evaluating them. (Watts 451–52)

A second text for the course was *Labor Attitudes and Problems* by W. E. Atkins and H. D. Laswell. A review published in the *University Journal of Business* called the book a "systematic and vivid presentation" of the material (rev. of *Labor Attitudes* 205). A reviewer of *The Worker in Modern Economic Society* (a third textbook) wrote that the material was well selected and that the book served a great need for a text that brought together strong scholarship that was scattered and hard to access (Weld 532). *Industrial Society* was also an assigned textbook in social economics. Another textbook intended for college courses, it contained contributions by leading economists, historians, and other social scientists of the time. One reviewer said of the text that it presupposed "a rather mature student mind and some background in social science" (Keister 421). A second reviewer offered a similar analysis of the text: "[T]aken as a whole, the book is conducted with skill and impartiality, though American first-year students must possess a high measure of intellectual acquisitiveness if they are prepared to assimilate the immense amount of complicated food these volumes provide" (Hobson 669).

The fifth (and final) text listed as a reading for social economics at Brookwood was *Principles of the New Economics*. A reviewer for the *American Economic Review* said of the book:

> As a matter of social perspective and psychological viewpoint the book is reasonably satisfactory, but as an economic analysis it is far from being adequate. It is very readable and interesting from start to finish; on the whole it is free from bias; and it does present to economists in a suggestive way the importance of using data made available in psychology. (Goodhue 625)

These reviews of the assigned texts for just one of Brookwood's "informational" courses make clear that the school assigned students college-level readings that were read and reviewed by scholars in their respective fields. Keeping in mind many of the workers attending Brookwood did not have strong education backgrounds, these readings would have been particularly challenging. Additionally, the reviews note the readings were not biased and provided the perspectives of a variety of scholars and researchers.

Alongside the "informational" courses at Brookwood, students also took several "tool" courses—courses focused on enabling students to put their knowledge into action. These courses included trade union administration technique, parliamentary law, English grammar, report making, labor journalism, public speaking, labor drama, and fieldwork preparation. These classes prepared students for and gave them practice in public speaking and debating; facilitating meetings; managing a union; writing labor news, editorials, and feature stories; composing union reports; analyzing and producing plays as a vehicle for informing audiences about labor issues and problems; evaluating strike situations and union organizing campaigns; implementing publicity methods; and facilitating strikes and food and clothing drives (*Brookwood Labor College*).

The textbooks listed under the second-year journalism course included Willard Grosvenor Bleyer's *Newspaper Writing and Editing* and *Special Feature Articles*, Matthew Lyle Spencer's *Editorial Writing*, George C. Bastian's *Editing the Day's News*, and John William Cunliffe and Gerhard R. Lomer's *Writing of Today* ("Books Used"). Bleyer, an associate professor of journalism at the University of Wisconsin, wrote his textbooks for use in college classes and claimed they were also accessible for those wishing to study journalism outside college (Bleyer v–vi). Spencer was a journalist, editor, administrator, and professor of journalism who published several journalism textbooks at the time. Bastian was a popular reporter, editor, and lecturer, and his book was designed for and used in introductory journalism courses. Cunliffe was professor of English and director of the School of Journalism at Columbia University. Lomer was an instructor in the English department at Columbia and later a librarian at McGill University. Their textbook was an edited collection of a variety of journal writing of the time, to be used as models.

These texts indicate that the Brookwood curriculum, in both the "informational" and the "tool" courses, used college-level, professional textbooks to inform and educate the students. The fact that these texts were primarily designed for general colleges and universities refutes, to some extent, accusations that the Brookwood curriculum was doctrinaire in its presentation of labor-related material. Important, also, is *how* this material was taught (discussed in the next section).

To complement the material covered by teachers in Brookwood courses, a number of outside speakers were brought in every year to lecture on "real-life" knowledge and experience with labor. A 1927 Executive Committee Report states the purpose of these actions: "to give the students the benefit not only of theoretical knowledge but the practical day to day work of the labor movement" (*Report of Brookwood Executive Committee* 3). According to a 1933–34 Brookwood report, the lectures of outside speakers fell into roughly four categories: "practical labor tactics, workers' education, political tendencies, and foreign affairs" (*Annual Report, 1933–34* 7). A 1930–31 report listed the following speakers for that year along with the topics they covered: a former editor of *The American Miner* (the industrial depression), an author (the situation in India), a professor from the University of Oslo (the labor movement of Norway), a playwright (labor drama), the director of the Workers Education Association in New Zealand (the Australian labor movement), a member of the Socialist Party (the role of the negro in the labor movement), and a traveler and writer (Russia) (*Annual Report, 1931–32*).

Similar to the knowledge disseminated by lyceums, the curriculum at Brookwood covered a broad range of topics. Different from the lyceums, though, Brookwood taught the content in relation to the labor movement, considered the content in depth, and taught students *how to apply* what they learned.

Learning to situate their labor experiences in a larger context likely helped students understand better their experiences, the causes and consequences of them, and alternative ways of thinking and acting based on them. As one student put it, "Before going to Brookwood, I could see only my own industry and state, but now I can see the whole labor movement—all unions, the unemployed, organized farmers, the whole country, the wider scope of labor's struggles" (*Brookwood's Contribution*).

The curriculum is also likely to have helped students become more confident communicators and leaders, evidenced by their reflections on their Brookwood education. One student wrote that "Brookwood training gave me more guts—more confidence on how to talk and not be bluffed or fooled by the bosses." Another student wrote, "After Brookwood I have been able to stand on two feet, answer questions and attacks. I didn't realize how helpful this would be until I got back into the thick of the fight" (*Brookwood's Contribution*). In addition, graduate Bessie Friedman wrote in the April 15, 1923, issue of the *Brookwood Review* that it was great to be back with fellow workers, "but this emotional feeling was accompanied by an intellectual stimulation. My two years in Brookwood had made me be self-confident; I had the knowledge of the background of the labor movement which my fellow workers lacked" (1). She also wrote,

> To my mind it is not enough to be emotionally stimulated and aware of a wrong situation. Militants as well as rank and filers ought to become clearly conscious of the policies and methods that an organization must pursue in order to succeed. (1)

According to archival documents, Brookwood's curriculum was challenging and multifaceted, blending theory and practice and addressing issues in both historical and contemporary contexts. The result was a more informed, more confident, and more experienced student body—a student body interested in and better equipped for engaging in intellectual activities, including those practiced in the Brookwood classroom.

TEACHING AND LEARNING PRACTICES

Influenced by John Dewey's educational philosophy of "learning by doing" and the progressive education movement, the founders of Brookwood intentionally avoided traditional, authoritative teaching practices and instead focused on a progressive, democratic pedagogy.[16] The belief was that teacher-student relations in the classroom reflected the political world outside: if students were passive and subservient in the classroom, they would also be so outside the classroom. Brookwood's teaching philosophy, then, situated students as active participants in a noncompetitive learning environment. It situated teachers as encouragers and facilitators of critical thinking, deliberation, and the expression of ideas—forms of intellectualism as this book seeks to define it. Faculty enacted this philosophy by using learning activities like discussion, debate, critical inquiry, collaboration, reading, writing, and speaking in their pedagogical practices. In a 1931 executive committee report, the authors wrote,

> Brookwood has stood for freedom in labor education. We have held that in our classrooms there must be the fullest freedom of discussion, willingness to face all sides of controverted subjects, a vigorous purpose to seek out the facts and to be guided by them. (*Report of Brookwood Executive Committee* 2)

Abraham Lefkowitz, a member of the board of directors concurred, writing, "Views, however radical or liberal, are not discouraged nor suppressed. Discussion is unlimited, opinions clash constantly on debatable questions" (57).

On paper, Brookwood leaders made explicit the school's emphasis on open-minded inquiry and analysis. For example, in a document titled *Suggested Brief Statement of Purpose* (1929), the authors stated,

> We want militant, radical workers, young people with vision and enthusiasm to come to Brookwood as well as more conservative trade unionists who are willing to study and analyze in an open-minded fashion the problems of life and of the labor movement in the modern world. (3)

Later in the document is a description of the educational policy of Brookwood:

> [E]ncouraging the full, free and critical discussion of all problems confronting the labor movement, the presentation of all points of view, including presentation of their viewpoints by spokesmen for various tendencies and parties in the movement, and encouragement in the students of a realistic attitude toward facts. (3)

Not surprisingly, then, the goal was "primarily to teach students how to think, not to tell them what to think" (*Brookwood Bulletin* 3)—contradictory to what critics have believed about education at U.S. labor colleges.

Brookwood course descriptions provide evidence that faculty did indeed design their courses to encourage critical thinking about course material. For example, Mark Starr's syllabus for his British Labor Movement course described the aim of the course as "to understand the main developments of the organized workers' movement in Great Britain and to analyze its present structure and ideals in comparison with the American movement." In the 1933–34 *Annual Report* for Brookwood, the teachers described their classes that year, citing a heavy emphasis on analysis and critical discussion. David J. Saposs explained history of the American Labor Movement this way:

> an analysis and description of the social and economic conditions that brought forth a working class and a labor movement, followed by a critical discussion by periods of all divisions, phases, ideas, and activities. . . . The course closes with an analysis of the most recent developments and an attempt to indicate possible future developments. (4)

Susan Shephard's dramatics course description stated students would read and analyze labor plays in order to prepare them to compose their own plays (6). Later in that report, in a section commenting on the quality and direction of the training, it stated, "In all our work this year Brookwood has tried to maintain and to encourage in the students a progressive, critical, and analytic approach to political, economic, and trade union policies . . ." (9). Clearly, the goal in these courses was to increase student understanding, but also to help develop students' ability to analyze and assess information.

Course assignments reveal some of the strategies teachers used to accomplish these goals. For example, a labor journalism assignment in Helen Norton's class asked students to read local labor papers and analyze the commercial advertisements. In a modern industry course, each lesson ended with "For Thought and Discussion" questions asking students what they think about what the text claims, what they noticed, and other things relating to the lesson. In the British Labor Movement course, Mark Starr asked students multiple questions, including, "Is the general strike an effective weapon and under what circumstances? Examine the tactics and the lack of agreement among the leaders" and "In 'Men and Machines' . . . Stuart Chase lists some of the causes of why the Industrial Revolution came first in England. Supplement these if you can and weigh their relative importance giving reasons for your placing." One assignment in Josephine Colby's report making course was for students to read convention proceedings, compare the arrangement and editing of the proceedings with the proceedings of the AFL, and then argue for which version they prefer, what they think works, and why. Such assignments indicate an emphasis on active engagement with course material.

Brookwood students were assigned reading in every course and were encouraged to read the texts available at the school's library.[17] Noted earlier, many of the readings were challenging texts, especially when we consider that many Brookwood students had limited educational experience and few had read such texts before. Harry Nilsson, a 1931 graduate of Brookwood, wrote in an essay titled "The Grads Come Through," "It is hard, at first, to get used to reading the books and magazines which are so new to most of the students" (27). In fact, according to Tucker P. Smith, Brookwood's director in 1936, figuring out what and how to teach workers was one of the most significant challenges the school faced because of students' poor preparation for such academic work (Smith 8). To facilitate the understanding, interpreting, and questioning of difficult material, teachers encouraged students to collaborate on their work[18] (Howlett 66). Teachers also consistently revised their courses and their methods to meet students' needs and abilities (Smith 8).

As the above assignments demonstrate, literacy activities were some of the most important learning tools used at Brookwood to encourage students' active engagement with ideas. (Reading, writing, and speaking were also skills taught at Brookwood as forms of activism, discussed in the next section.) Susan Kates, in her analysis of some of the same Brookwood archival documents, concluded that those instructors at Brookwood teaching "rhetorical study"[19] intentionally used reading, writing, and speaking assignments to help students understand and interrogate their marginalized standing (1). They also taught students to consider the way language gets used in different contexts (78). In her words, "Reading, writing, and speaking about their employment experiences gave Brookwood students the opportunity to gain a critical perspective on the forces that threatened their lives and well-being" (96). According to Kates, these features of writing and speaking instruction did not typically appear in the curricula of more traditional institutions of the time (77, 86).

The result of such "activist education" (as Kates termed it) was students who could not only serve the labor movement as good speakers and writers, but students who could think critically about language, rhetoric, and communication. Students put these skills to use outside the classroom when they wrote memoranda to Brookwood teachers and administrators and when they participated in the meetings and discussions about the program mentioned earlier.

Reinforcing claims that Brookwood taught students how to think critically are students' and observers' accounts of the Brookwood experience. Former student Mary Goff said in 1924 that in history classes students were not trained to memorize facts but to analyze critically and openly the forces and conditions behind historical events. "We do not feel that great barrier between the instructor and the students. We ask questions freely and when we have opinions we express them. We are stimulated to ask, to find out, to dig ourselves . . ." (ctd. in Howlett 65). One student wrote in the February 1932 issue of the *Brookwood Review*, that classes were "conducted an [*sic*] a discussion basis with reading assignments and written reports to amplify and crystallize the classroom work" (4). Henry Harap, a professor of education at Case Western, observed at Brookwood in 1923 that

> the class recitations are friendly and informal. The students discussed and asked questions with a view to getting information rather than to show up their intelligence. . . . The class meets as a Seminar rather than as a lecture or recitation group. The students coming out of industry or Trade Unions bring to the discussion information out of their practical experience. . . . The students do not appear to take what the instructors say as Gospel. They have a wholesome, constructive, critical attitude. (ctd. in Howlett 64)

Similarly, President Farrell of the Kansas State College of Agriculture and Applied Science commented in 1930 on Brookwood students' interactions with guest speakers, noting they asked "numerous, pertinent, and well worded" questions, subjecting the speaker to "a critical examination" (ctd. in Clark 402).

The learning and thinking activities utilized in the Brookwood classroom (including discussion, debate, analysis, collaboration, reading, writing, and speaking) increased students' engagement with ideas and nurtured a desire to engage in critical discussions not just in the classroom, but also outside it. One example of this is students' participation as writers and editors of the school paper (started by labor journalism teacher Helen Norton) and their creation of other student publications. As described in a 1924 Brookwood report, the school paper was not necessarily seen as only a place to practice the art of labor journalism (noted in the next section), but as a discussion forum: "The paper will aim to provide an opportunity for the discussion of problems of workers' education, including particularly problems of teaching method" (*Report to the Second International Conference* 7).

Demonstrating their desire to engage with others in writing and their sense of initiative or motivation, students started and maintained a number of other student-run publications over the years. One of them, the *Brookwood Fellowship Review,* was written and published by alumni of Brookwood and contained book reviews, quotes, reports, updates, articles by graduates, and faculty news.[20] The purpose of the publication was recorded in the first edition:

> The first and most important function of the *Fellowship Review* is to be a medium for shop talk among Brookwood graduates. . . . It should never get to looking so presentable that our real problems and sincere opinions do not get an airing. Within the *Fellowship* we should seek to build up a community of understanding and a free critical spirit. (10)

The fact that this publication existed is evidence of students' ongoing (post-graduation) desire for critical engagement and expression of opinions. This work demonstrates students' desire to engage with others in writing, their ability to think independently, and their sense of initiative and motivation.

Faculty modeled critical thinking and intellectual engagement and inquiry not only in their teaching practices but also in their research and in their continued participation in labor movement activities. Faculty at Brookwood were known to participate in protests and help with union work, and they published their research in the form of books, textbooks, articles, and pamphlets. In fact, Brookwood was "no sheltered retreat where professors sit spinning theories in slippered ease" (*Twelfth Anniversary Review* 5).

The atmosphere of open, critical inquiry and debate in the Brookwood classroom was supported by the absence of grades, exams, and diplomas as incentives for education, creating an environment of collaborative, noncompetitive learning. Students helped each other learn and shared their knowledge through discussions and debates both in and out of the classroom. This atmosphere, along with the teaching and learning practices Brookwood utilized and encouraged, helped students become active, critical learners both inside and outside the classroom.

EDUCATION FOR ACTIVISM

Brookwood's organizational structure, curriculum, and classroom practices were designed for one overarching practical purpose: to make students effective activists for the labor movement. Based on what we know from students' comments on their autobiographical essays, they already were or were at least interested in being labor activists. What difference, then, did the Brookwood program make in students' activism? According to archival documents from the school, the program helped students see and perform fieldwork with a greater understanding of the social, cultural, political, and economic issues that influenced laborers and the labor movement. It also taught them different forms of activism (including labor journalism and labor drama) that were new to most of them. Additionally, the program made students more effective activists by teaching them how to communicate and analyze information. The great significance of these outcomes, in relation to the intellectual influence of Brookwood, was that students' activist work positioned them not only as intellectual participants but also as sponsors of intellectualism—spreading to others knowledge, class-consciousness, an interest in learning, and the desire to critically engage with ideas. This positioning of students as activists was unique among educational institutions of the time, adding to Brookwood's significance in fostering public intellectualism in the twentieth century. The two most popular and successful forms of activism performed by students and graduates were labor journalism and labor drama.

Labor Journalism

Mentioned earlier, some Brookwood courses were designed to help students improve their writing for the purpose of communicating with and persuading an audience. In the 1933–34 *Annual Report*, Susan M. Shepherd noted that in her grammar and writing course the focus was on getting students to "express themselves effectively on paper" by reviewing grammar, punctuation, and other elements, and practicing various types of writing. A speaking and writing course concentrated on improving students' skills in "public discussion," grammar, spelling, and the writing of reports, minutes, resolutions, and promotional materials (*Brookwood Bulletin* 8–9).

Students in Josephine Colby's English class learned how to write pamphlets after studying existing pamphlets. Helen Norton taught her labor journalism students about the power of writing and how to use it to communicate effectively and persuade an audience, including using illustrations and vernacular familiar to the target audience (Colby). Her course notes reveal she told them the purpose of labor journalism is threefold: "To spread labor news," "To put into simple, readable form such material as research findings or complicated labor agreements and measures," and "To influence opinion and feeling, both among workers and the general public." Combined, these courses taught students to use rhetoric and literacy skills in their activist work.

The importance placed on these skills is indicated by the amount of hours devoted to these classes. For example, labor journalism was a course that met for three hours weekly for the whole year and speaking and writing met for five hours a week for the entire year. By comparison, American history, modern industry, and basic industries were three-hour-a-week courses that met for only half of the year.

Part of what made Brookwood so effective was that students received more than just training in writing to communicate and persuade; they were given the opportunity to practice it. Labor journalism instructor Helen Norton started the *Brookwood Review* in 1922 to provide a real space for students and teachers to practice their journalism skills. Written, edited, and published by teachers and students, the *Review* was typically published monthly and contained reports on labor issues, strikes, and problems; short reports of speakers visiting Brookwood; descriptions of institutes held at Brookwood; reports on incoming, current, or past students and teachers; book reviews of books about labor issues; student activity in strikes and drama performances; changes in curriculum and classes; and creative stories about the lives of workers.

Writing for this publication helped students understand the use of writing for activism purposes. In the January 1, 1924, issue, student Charles Moore wrote, "It seems impossible to set bounds to the influence of the press. . . . The newspaper is a social benefit or a social menace according to the motive of the people who control it." In the same issue, student Ben Thomas wrote, "The study of Journalism makes its importance apparent, in view of the fact that the press is one of the powerful propagnda [*sic*] agents of the employing class." Students' recognition of the power of writing to educate and persuade an audience made writing more than a tool for their own learning; it became a tool they could use to educate others.

Labor Drama

One of the most significant developments in the labor college curriculum was the addition of labor drama. Representative of an early twentieth-century movement by Progressive reformers to use theater as a form of mass education (Kett 321), drama was introduced experimentally at Brookwood in fall 1925. Labor drama was added to the Brookwood curriculum to teach students to analyze and produce plays in an effort to educate and raise the consciousness of audiences about labor through entertainment.

By 1934 theater was thoroughly integrated into the activities of Brookwood, with yearly Labor Chautauqua tours funded by the school. According to a 1934 press release, in two months the program had ninety performances in eight states, reaching more than twenty-two thousand people. Performances were financed by ticket sales, collections, contributions from individuals and groups, and were sometimes underwritten by union or labor organizations (*Brookwood Labor Players*).

The 1931–32 *Brookwood Bulletin and Announcement of Labor Courses* described the labor drama class as "analysis and production of plays as a vehicle of labor expression." Students received training in writing, acting, and directing plays, and in the construction of simple stage settings. Students were also taught the history of labor drama. A handout from Elizabeth English's 1935–36 dramatics class, titled "On Reading and Writing Plays," stated that though students were not expected to produce masterpieces, they would learn how to use their labor and union experiences to write effective plays. In this way, literacy practices were central to the Brookwood curriculum and to students' expression of ideas for activism purposes.

Because labor plays written by students and teachers were fashioned after their own personal experiences and presented the challenges and problems most present in their lives, these courses also used reading, writing, and speech to help students process and present their own labor experiences. The topics of students' and teachers' labor plays included a textile strike, a tragedy in the coal fields, the campaign to unionize sweatshops in the garment industry, the story of a union leader who remained true to the cause despite losing his wife on the picket line, the GM auto strike, the positive results of workers protesting collectively, an antiwar drama about young textile workers striking instead of making gun cotton, an account of a union that got the boss who avoided paying his workers, and issues of racism, sexism, and poor job conditions. The labor plays written and performed by Brookwood students reflect a national trend beginning in the 1930s: the politicization of theater (Altenbaugh, "Proletarian Drama" 197).

Brookwood documents indicate labor drama was a successful tool for educating audiences about labor conditions and problems and got audiences interested in labor issues and in joining the cause for social change. According to the 1931–32 Brookwood *Annual Report*, "After every performance [of the play *Mill Shadows*] people hung around asking questions about working conditions as typified in the play and about Brookwood." Audiences were often stirred to do more than join the cause. A Brookwood Labor Players brochure claimed that after seeing one of the labor plays, the audience members often sought advice on how to create their own drama group. In these ways, student performers fostered intellectualism among the audience members. Their work as activists interested and motivated others to engage with the social, cultural, and political issues affecting laborers.

These plays educated the participants as well. An *Annual Report* claimed students and staff considered the time and energy they devoted to their labor drama work worthwhile. A press release from Brookwood in 1934 argued the trips gave students valuable experience with workers outside the school that they could take back to their local situations. In her book *Staging Strikes: Workers' Theatre and the American Labor Movement*, Colette A. Hyman argued that "in participating in such projects, students could develop self-confidence and public-speaking skills while they explored problems of labor relations and labor organizing" (22).

In the *Fifteenth Anniversary Review* of Brookwood, John W. Martindale wrote this about the value of labor drama at Brookwood:

> These Chautauqua tours are not just a stunt, nor a way of giving our students a sight-seeing tour. They are a very important part of Brookwood's total program of workers' education. They are educational for both the students and for the audience. The students profit by the examination they make of the issues and situations about which they write the plays, by the self-confidence and stage presence which result from repeated appearances before an audience, and by intimate contact with a significant portion of the American labor movement. As for the audience, it is obvious that they will not get as thorough an understanding of current problems as they might from a regular study class. Brookwood carries on such classes in the field wherever they can be organized. But hundreds of workers who will not come to a class will come to see a show. They will not only learn something; they will also get an emotional drive which will make them want to do something about it. (44)

Experience with labor journalism and labor drama educated students, taught them analytical and rhetorical skills, and educated their audiences. Additionally, they both made knowledge more accessible to their audiences. This is where the Brookwood experience seems to come full circle. Brookwood worked to make education accessible to workers; in turn, it trained workers to make education accessible to the public. Like the entertaining and instructive performances on the lyceum stage, the labor drama labor colleges provided made education pleasurable and entertaining. It is not surprising that (as Altenbaugh claimed) labor drama was the most successful and profitable part of Brookwood (*Education* 228).

While some may argue that making knowledge entertaining and accessible is a form of "dumbing down," I argue that making knowledge accessible and engaging serves a greater purpose—getting people interested. In the end, the activism Brookwood prepared students for and engaged them in placed students in the role of educator and in the role of cultivating intellectualism in others. Through their activism work (based heavily on their reading, writing, and oral performance of texts), students had the opportunity to motivate their audiences to learn, to think critically, and to take action.

ACCESS TO BROOKWOOD

Like lyceums, labor colleges were designed to provide education to a portion of the population that had little or less access to more traditional (and more reputable) educational institutions. Unlike lyceums, labor colleges (and Brookwood in particular) were designed to serve a very specific, limited population: adult laborers and labor movement leaders. As stated in a 1927 memorandum, to be accepted into Brookwood's program, students had to have worked in industry[21] and held membership in a labor union for a minimum of one year. They were also required to have three references, of whom two had to speak to their loyalty to organized labor. No particular prior education was compulsory for students (*Memorandum on Entrance Requirements*). In fact, we know from a 1927 census of Brookwood that students' previous education ranged from college training to very little public schooling: four students had no public school education, a little over one-half went no further than grade school, and only half of these completed the full eight years (*A Census*).[22]

Reflecting on the first ten years of Brookwood, the executive committee stated in a report:

> It is important that Brookwood has had its doors open from the beginning to students irrespective of nationality, race, creed, or color, or their economic and political views and affiliations, and that it has sought to maintain in its own community that spirit of brotherhood and comradeship which we trust will be universal in a nobler social order when economic classes have been wiped out. (*Report of Brookwood Executive Committee* 2)

Efforts were made, also, to maintain a representative student body, keeping in mind the industries that students were coming from, their union participation, and their geographic location in the country. The rationale was that a student body with varied points of view would enhance the educational experience, and would represent the reality of the labor movement (*Memorandum on Entrance Requirements* 2). Like lyceums, labor colleges prided themselves on being highly accessible, claiming they did not discriminate based on age, race, or gender. Also like the lyceums, though, access to labor colleges *was* complicated by issues of cost, affiliation, race, and gender.

According to Altenbaugh, some critics have called labor colleges "elitist" and "expensive" (*Education* 4) because the cost affected who was able to attend. In a 1934 acceptance letter from Brookwood to Leon A. Cousens, the cost per student for a year was listed as $200 for board, room, and laundry. Rarely did (or could) students afford to pay this cost themselves. Most often, students were funded by a labor organization or by individual donations to the school. Some, however, could not find the money or sponsorship to attend. Others could not afford to spend two years away from work or from their families. In addition to cost, the work experience and loyalty to organized labor required of students limited who could attend. Combined, this means that despite a relatively open admissions policy, Brookwood really only educated students who could afford to leave their family and jobs and who were already dedicated to the labor movement.

A survey of current and past students from 1921 to 1931 conducted by Helen G. Norton's 1931 class provides further details about who actually attended Brookwood. According to the survey, 186 students attended Brookwood during the first decade. Of them, 25.8 percent were native whites, 39.7 percent were native whites of foreign parentage, 31.7 percent were foreign-born whites, and 3.2 percent were of other races. Men made up the majority at 61 percent; 39 percent were women. Students came from twenty-seven states and seven foreign countries and from thirty-five different labor unions. The median age was twenty-six (*A Survey of Brookwood*). These data show that though Brookwood was designed to be accessible, very few nonwhites attended. In fact, only five African American students attended Brookwood in those ten years. This is due, in part, to black students only beginning to be admitted in 1925, and to the NAACP being one of the only organizations offering black students financial support (Altenbaugh, *Education* 142).

Following the entrance of black students to Brookwood, the school's administration sought out black speakers who could speak to labor issues. A 1927 report mentioned that a number of "negroes" presented at the school that year (*Report of Brookwood Executive Committee* 3). A letter to Robert W. Bagnall of the NAACP in 1929 inviting him to speak at an upcoming symposium at Brookwood stated, "We are very anxious that . . . our students should have an opportunity to hear a number of negro leaders in the field of labor organization, civil liberties, inter-racial relations, etc." (Muste). In addition, though women were clearly admitted to Brookwood's program and made up about 40 percent of attendees, very few became prominent leaders in the labor movement (Kates 93). This is, of course, consistent with gender issues of the time in American culture at large. Consequently, to some extent labor colleges (similar to lyceums) contributed to traditional notions that intellectualism is something for white men who could "afford" to engage in learning activities.

Despite access to labor colleges being complicated by cost, affiliation, race, and gender, Brookwood worked to make knowledge accessible to those who could not participate in the full two-year program. Beginning in 1924 Brookwood started offering summer school short courses. These courses consisted of twelve days of intensive training in classes with titles such as "Your Job and Your Pay," "Principles of Unionism," "Public Speaking and Parliamentary Law," "Labor Publicity," "Economics," "Labor Problems," and "English/Labor Journalism." In 1928, Brookwood established an official extension department. The extension department offered correspondence courses on various topics, including, for example, "Modern Industrial Problems," "Public Speaking, Labor History," and "Trade Union Problems and Policies." As a brochure for the correspondence courses stated, the cost for seven to fourteen lessons ranged from five to fifteen dollars—much more affordable for many laborers at the time. The instructors provided outlines and suggestions for reading and study, writing assignments, and gave each student feedback on their work (*Correspondence Courses for Workers*). In addition to correspondence courses, Brookwood began offering short institutes at the school and "class circuits," which were classes that met once a week in surrounding towns (Martindale, "Carrying" 24).

The extension program also supplied speakers and educational assistance to trade unions, labor colleges and classes, cooperative societies, YWCA, industrial clubs, discussion groups, and other groups and individuals (ctd. in Altenbaugh, *Education* 126). The program was indeed extensive, reaching workers in Philadelphia, Harrisburg, Lancaster, and York, Pennsylvania; Newark and Paterson, New Jersey; Durham and Greensboro, North Carolina; and Baltimore, Maryland (127). In 1931 Brookwood began to offer a one-year program for those unable to attend for the full two years. The primary reason for this change, stated in a 1931 report by the executive committee, was making the knowledge more accessible and more quickly enactable. The rationale was worded this way:

> We have desired to get more graduates out into the movement, after a shorter separation from their unions and from industry, with a more intensive though less extended course in the subjects chiefly required by men and women who are to be useful in the difficult and perplexing American labor scene of this present period. (*Report of Brookwood Executive Committee* 2)

Another way Brookwood attempted to make education accessible to others was through its pamphlet series. According to a 1934 press release, these inexpensive pamphlets were "designed to present important ideas and facts about the labor movement in a clear and simple manner in terms of workers' experience." They were intentionally written with a simple sentence structure and vocabulary for "rank and file workers who find most reading on economics and labor problems difficult work." Among the subjects of the pamphlets were "What a union did for the coal miners," "Important Union methods," "How a Trade Union is Run," "Our Labor Movement Today," and "Why Bother about the Government?" (*The Brookwood Labor Pamphlets*). Fitting Brookwood's educational philosophy and design, the pamphlets not only disseminated information but spurred discussion with a series of questions and reading suggestions at the end. The questions often included both larger critical questions and more specific personal ones.

Like lyceums, American labor colleges were not accessible to all. Participation in labor colleges was limited to those who could get funding and time away from jobs and family, and to those with the required amount of work and labor union experience. Despite these limitations, Brookwood broadened education for laborers in the twentieth century. And those who did gain access to Brookwood's program experienced a curriculum and environment that encouraged an interest in learning, critical thinking, the valuing of education, and educating others through activism—supporting and fostering intellectualism in students.

Though archival documents from Brookwood Labor College cannot tell us everything about each student's experience there or about the exact consequences or results of programs like Brookwood's, the story they tell is that Brookwood provided its students a breadth of informational, historical, and theoretical knowledge related to labor issues of the time along with the opportunity to practice and improve skills that would make them more effective critical thinkers, communicators, and labor leaders. Despite this success, Brookwood closed its doors in 1937, and other labor colleges followed, failing to accomplish their central goal: to build a new social order.[23] A number of factors led to Brookwood's closing in 1937: fragmentation of the political left (including a majority of the participants and supporters), financial problems stemming from the Great Depression, and Brookwood's independence (and consequent lack of an outside funding source).

While the dream of a new social order was never realized for Brookwood and other labor colleges, they did succeed in educating students and engaging them in the theory and practice of the labor movement. Noted in the *Twelfth Anniversary Review* of Brookwood,

> Education is not confined to "book larnin" at Brookwood. These workers study economics and trade unionism, history and economic geography, public speaking and journalism, but the most effective education comes out of the exchange of experiences and ideas with workers from other industries and other parts of the country. (10)

The importance placed on enacting what they learned and on a lifelong commitment to educating others is evident in the work students did after leaving Brookwood. The *Fifteenth Anniversary Review* program listed the following about Brookwood graduates:

> Eighty-four of us have recently participated in strikes or organization campaigns; 54 have held full time positions in unions; 49 have been arrested for labor activity; 65 have written for or edited labor papers; 76 have taught workers' classes and organized workers' education centers; 74 have been active in labor political organizations; 41 have helped in the organization of the unemployed; 17 have taken part in the consumers' cooperative movement; and the same number have worked in farm organizations. (28)

This evidence that students continued to engage and participate in the labor movement after leaving the program helps demonstrate the desire, motivation, and dedication students had, not only to the movement but also to educating and helping others. Consequently, the influence labor colleges had on the intellectualism of those who participated was significant. Despite criticisms of education for a practical purpose, acquiescent workers, and the spread of useful knowledge, an examination of the students, the institutional structure, the curriculum, the classroom, and the activism at Brookwood Labor College reveals that intellectualism was practiced at Brookwood in a variety of forms and was supported by an atmosphere conducive to the desire for and pursuit of knowledge.

One possible effect of reimagining intellectualism in a way that recognizes the intellectual import of the learning that took place at Brookwood and other labor colleges that have long functioned as the educational base of the labor movement is that it could help reframe contemporary views of unions and laborers as inherently non- or anti-intellectual. In fact, it is telling that just recently National Labor College (NLC) in Silver Spring, Maryland,[24] closed its doors following the spring 2014 semester. NLC was established in 1969 to, much like Brookwood, provide "physical and intellectual space for the labor movement" and prepare union members, leaders, and workers for the political and social challenges they face. According to the NLC website, the school closed due to "financial exigencies" (*National Labor College*). A revaluing of the intellectual work at Brookwood and a broader view of intellectualism today could shed new light on the recent work of NLC and contemporary unions.

The next chapter, which looks closely at GED writing workshops in the twenty-first century, builds on the issues highlighted by an examination of the lyceum and Brookwood Labor College by probing in more depth the relationship between basic literacy education and intellectualism. In addition, the qualitative research methods employed in this most contemporary case study allowed for a more in-depth exploration of the complexity of individual participants' perspectives on these issues.

chapter four

INTELLECTUALISM AND BASIC LITERACY EDUCATION

Twenty-First-Century GED Writing Workshops

THE LINDBERG CENTER[1] IS A neighborhood nonprofit institution in the Midwest that has been providing programs designed to promote economic advancement, self-sufficiency, and leadership among youth and adults for over a century. Among the programs the center offers is a combined GED and Adult Basic and Literacy Education (ABLE) class designed to prepare students for the GED exam. The GED/ABLE program offers three-hour workshops three times a week covering the various subjects on the GED exam. In 2003 the center formed a partnership with a nearby university, for which graduate students collaborate with the center to design and teach a sequence of six three-hour writing workshops three times a year to help students prepare for the writing portion of the GED exam. Like lyceums and labor colleges, the GED writing workshops at the Lindberg Center provide access to education for adults who, due to their personal or economic circumstances, have not completed or had access to other forms of secondary or higher education. Also like lyceums and labor colleges, it serves people typically not categorized as intellectual.

Because traditional views of intellectualism conflate it with academics and academic success, with "highbrow" literacy practices, and with learning for its own sake, basic literacy education programs like the Lindberg Center's writing workshops fall under the rubric of nonintellectual and are consequently overlooked in discussions of American intellectualism. Viewed through the perspective of the more inclusive definition of intellectualism suggested in this book, however, these workshops can be recognized as a site and sponsor of intellectualism in the twenty-first century. It is important to recognize the intellectual experiences of students like those at the Lindberg Center because, as Mike Rose has argued, "second chance" education institutions are typically discussed in public only in terms of their economic benefits. If we fail to look beyond economic benefits and recognize the ways of thinking and engaging with ideas that these types of institutions foster, then we may also fail to "create the conditions" needed to foster such intellectual work (*Back to School* 77).

My research at the Lindberg Center intentionally focused specifically on the writing workshops, because as a form of basic literacy education they allow us to more closely understand and complicate the presumed disconnect between intellectualism and basic literacy education—an issue of great concern to the field of rhetoric, composition, and literacy studies. In an effort to study the intellectual import of this site of twenty-first-century adult basic literacy education, I observed two sections of a six-week sequence of the writing workshops (a day class and a night class), surveyed and interviewed students, and interviewed workshop instructors and the program supervisor.[2] At first, I asked students on a volunteer basis to anonymously complete a written survey asking them about their educational experiences and beliefs, their opinions about the workshops, and their literacy practices. Between the two classes I received fifteen completed surveys.[3] Following the surveys, I interviewed (again on a volunteer basis) thirteen current students and one former student. During the interviews, I asked students more detailed questions about their past and present education experiences, their attitudes toward and interest in learning and literacy, their assessment of the writing workshops, and their beliefs about intelligence and intellectualism. In my interviews with the instructors and program supervisor, I inquired about the goals and objectives for the workshops, their perceptions of the students' work and motivations for learning, and their interpretations of the educational environment of the workshops.

Responses to the surveys and interviews, along with my own observations of the twelve workshops, shed light on students' attitudes toward learning and education and their engagement with the work they were doing in the workshops—characteristics central to a revised definition of intellectualism that reflects the qualities we value in our discussions of the purpose of education. Based on my interactions with students and teachers at the Lindberg Center, I argue that a majority of the students came to the workshops interested, motivated learners who value education. In addition, the literacy activities used in these workshops encouraged and supported students' interest in education and fostered their critical engagement with ideas. These findings challenge the notion that basic or remedial literacy programs—and their participants—cannot be intellectual.

THE STUDENTS

According to the program supervisor, the Lindberg Center students are typically twenty-five to forty years old, unemployed or making low wages, and on some form of public assistance. A majority of the students are African American, many are single parents, and most have tried to get their GED through other programs or at other times in their lives. Most dropped out of school somewhere between eighth and eleventh grade and start the program at the center testing at a fourth- or fifth-grade level. The students I interviewed reflect a similar profile. They range in age from nineteen to sixty. Six were men and eight were women, and all but one identified his or her race as Black; one woman identified her race as Somali. While most dropped out of school between tenth and twelfth grade, a few left between seventh and ninth grade. The primary reasons cited for dropping out of school were having a baby, lack of support (family, economic, school), low self-esteem, or the need to work. Table 4.1 provides a brief look at the demographics and experiences of the fourteen students I interviewed.

I begin my analysis of the Lindberg Center as a site of intellectualism with a close look at the students' beliefs about education, their motivations for furthering their education, and their views of intelligence and intellectualism.

Beliefs about Education and Motivations for Learning

Students' motivation to learn was evident not only in their performance during the workshops but it was also demonstrated by their willingness to voluntarily devote nine hours a week to their GED training (three hours for the writing workshop and six hours for training in other subjects), often balancing this with a full-time labor-intensive job or raising a family, or both. Understanding their motivations helps us understand better their beliefs about education and learning, and consequently what fuels their

Table 4.1. Writing Workshop Student Interviewees

Name	*Age*	*When Dropped Out of School*	*Why Dropped Out of School*	*Why Working on GED*
			Women	
Anna	54	10th grade	Had a couple children; couldn't read	For pride
Carin	50s	9th grade	Dysfunctional family; racism in school; had to start working at age 15	To handle things better; because she believes knowledge is power
Dina	45	12th grade	Low self-esteem; had a baby	To gain self-esteem; to demonstrate to children and grandchildren she can do it
Jackie	30s	At age 17	Had daughter at 14; pregnant again at 17	For a better life
Kim	20s	At age 17	Became pregnant	To better self; to get a better job; to be a role model to her children
LaShonda	28	9th/10th grade	Didn't get much help from teachers so lost interest	Wants a better life; employment; help nieces and nephews
Sara	19	Didn't drop out	Completed high school but couldn't pass the science portion of the state's required graduation test	To go to college
Teresa	29/30	10th grade	Hanging out with a bad crowd	To better herself and her kids
			Men	
Carl	early 20s	10th or 11th grade	Behavior issues	For better job opportunities; to improve living situation; to be a role model
Jerome	20s	11th grade	Skipping school; lack of interest	For a better life via a better job
Joseph	25	10th grade	Needed to work to take care of himself because his family couldn't	To go to college
Malcolm	27	After completing 8th grade	Always struggled with school; a lot of depression and insecurity	Self-confidence; because education is a tool; because it's a burden on his back
Wendell	60	7th grade	Racism; no motivational help from home; back and forth to jail at age 13; doctor labeled him retarded	To prove something to self and others
William	26	2 weeks before high school graduation	Got in trouble; economic problems	To go to college and self-respect

participation in this GED program. The three main forces motivating students that surfaced in the interviews were the belief that education increases access to things they want, self-esteem, and an awareness of the effect their lack of education has on others.

All of the students I interviewed value education because they assume it leads to a better life. What students mean by "a better life" varies, of course. For some, a better life means a better job, more money, a nice home, or the opportunity for more education for themselves or their children. For others, a better life means a nice life for their children, having the respect of others, or believing in themselves. For Kim, a career as a surgical tech and owning a house are among the things she wants but believes she can't get without a GED. Her statement about why she values education is indicative of many of the students' responses: "You need [education] to do anything that you wanna do . . . it's like I have all these goals I wanna do but I have to get my GED first before I do that." In Joseph's words, "Education is life pretty much . . . without it you pretty much can't live." For Wendell, the purpose of education is "so you can educate yourself so you can have a better future, so you can have a better life, especially black people because we have had such a hard time." Cate, the program supervisor, said that from what she has seen, students make this connection because of their "real-world" experiences in which their lack of education has limited access to things they have wanted.

In addition to associating education with access, all interviewees indicated their interests in and motivations for furthering their education are tied to self-respect and overcoming feelings of inadequacy. For instance, when I asked Dina, a forty-five-year-old woman working part-time at McDonald's, why she's working on her GED now, she said, "I hope to gain self-esteem, definitely, number one." Likewise, Wendell, the oldest person in the program at the time at age sixty, said, "I'm motivated to do it now, not because it will do me any good at this age. I just wanna say to myself, and I got brothers and sisters I can say to, I did get this." Anna, a fifty-four-year-old mother of ten, said, "The hat and gown is basically what I'm here for. I wanna walk around with the little tassels at the store, butt naked with the hat on . . . ya know, just be proud of it." In her interview, the program supervisor said she has observed in students the connection between their self-esteem and getting the GED. For many, she said, it's about proving to themselves they can *earn* the diploma, rather than have it handed to them.

While students like Anna, Wendell, and Dina are motivated to get their GED primarily by a desire to prove something to themselves, for other students self-esteem is one of a number of benefits (and perhaps not the main benefit). For Teresa, a single mother with a full-time clerical job at a doctor's office, among the forces motivating her is her desire to feel more adequate in situations like talking to her kids' teachers and in interviewing for jobs. She described a meeting she had recently had with her son's teacher:

> The teacher was talking to me like a one-on-one situation and I'm like okay, what is you saying. Tell me, explain to me a little more so I know what you're talking bout cause I didn't know the definition of the word that came out of her mouth. And I felt kinda stupid like okay, you're a parent now, why don't you know what this means.

Teresa's hope, then, is that with more education she'll be able to understand the teacher better because she'll have more knowledge. For Malcolm, with education comes confidence (a confidence he admits he is lacking): "If you can speak correctly, you can carry yourself correctly. . . . I just think education gives you a confidence . . . like hey, I can do this. I can conquer anything in the world." William, too, said self-esteem is one of his motivations because

> there's a lot of people like my friends and other people that I've met along the line that look down on me. I don't have a high school diploma so they feel that I don't really matter and I'm not doing anything in life.

Based on students' comments, many of them are also motivated by their understanding of the relationship between their education and the lives of others. This is seen, for example, in Kim's concern about not being smarter than her fifth-grade daughter, LaShonda's desire to help her nieces and nephews with their schoolwork, Carl's desire to be a role model for his brother and his race, and Dina's aspiration to be a role model for her grandkids. Teresa said,

> Ya know, I have two young sons and I don't want them coming to me asking me questions I can't answer cause I don't know. . . . I wanna be this good parent and good role model for my sons.

One of the most striking comments in response to the question of why they were working to attain their GED came on the anonymous survey. One student wrote, "I wanna give my family a better man." This comment demonstrates well students' beliefs that improving themselves can benefit others. This sentiment, for many, relates back to their belief that education equals access. Many of the students spoke about wanting to further their education so they could provide better for their families.

My interviews with students and teachers also revealed that for most students, their interest in education increased with age. Many students spoke of not really caring about their education when they were younger, but age and experience changed that. When I asked Dina what's different about then from now, she said, "I'm older. I'm a little wiser. I know I need that education to go further. And, I'd say my self-esteem is much better." Kim said when she was younger she didn't think that as she got older her education would be so important. Even Carl, who was only twenty at the time of the interview, spoke of a change that came with age. He said, "As you mature and get older you start to think and look at the finer things in life and not the faster things in life." The instructor of the evening workshops said that most of the older students are extremely focused—they write and write and write and repeatedly ask for feedback. It's the younger ones, he said, who sometimes struggle to stay focused and who write a paragraph and then stop. What these comments reveal is that students' interest in education and their willingness to engage in intellectual activities came with the awareness that they needed it to get some of the things they desire, and this awareness came with experience and maturity.

Students' belief that education will necessarily improve their lives is based on a conviction similar to the literacy myth: the belief that the acquisition of literacy by itself is necessary for—and necessarily leads to—economic, social, and cognitive advancement (Graff, *The Literacy Myth* xxxvi–xxxviii). In this case, students assume their lack of education has been a barrier (or, in Teresa's words, "a burden on my shoulders") holding them back from a good life or from being the person they want to be. Students' interest in and commitment to furthering their education, then, is significantly tied to their belief that education will necessarily open access to the things in life they desire. This can be seen, too, in what was absent from students' discussions of what motivates them to get their GED. None of them ever mentioned what specific content or skills they thought they should learn. Their assumption is that their lack of education has been a barrier and the solution is education. That education, however, seems general, or at least not clearly defined.

Students' belief that education is necessary for—and necessarily leads to—a "better life" has likely been fostered by messages they receive from society and from educational institutions, including the Lindberg Center itself. On paper, the center perpetuates the belief that education leads to advancement, evidenced by its vision statement claiming the mission is to empower students by "reducing barriers to and increasing education, employment, and life skills." Because "reducing barriers" is synonymous with increasing access, what this vision implies is that, at least in theory, increasing access to education, employment, and life skills empowers students and opens doors for them. Some students' belief in this "education myth" of sorts also appears to have been cultivated by family. For example, Carin stated, "My brother tells me all the time knowledge is power." Carl said his grandmother inspired him to learn, instilling in him the importance of education. William said his parents and pastor encourage him to get his GED because "they think that I can do better in life."

While the belief that education in general will increase access to the things you desire can (and does) help motivate learners, it can also be dangerous. As Harvey J. Graff demonstrated in *The Literacy Myth*, the belief that literacy is an independent variable that can by itself "equalize things" and "reduce barriers" overlooks the influence of a host of other complicating factors that affect equality and access, including race, class, gender, and ethnicity. The myth that education in general can have the same effect can lead to the same issue. In fact, people use such myths to argue against social programs like welfare and Affirmative Action, claiming that if people have access to education and literacy, it's their own fault if they don't have what they need. It's interesting to think here about Wendell's comment that education can lead to a better life "especially [for] black people." Earlier in his interview he referenced not having received a good education because he went to school "when there was a lot of racism goin' on" and "black children didn't get the proper education that we should have gotten." Acknowledging he didn't receive a good education because of his race, he still assumes education can necessarily lead to a better life for him and others.

If students themselves buy in to the myth that education necessarily "equalizes things," they may blame themselves or their lack of education for their economic and social circumstances and overlook other social and cultural factors that have affected their educational experiences or have created barriers in their lives. This may lead to students assuming that once they get their GED, some or all of the barriers may be removed. As Graff's research showed, however, "Literacy's role . . . was rarely direct or independent; it did not counteract the dominant patterns of inequality but largely reinforced them" (87). Students' GEDs also likely would not.

The Lindberg Center students' belief that education equals access is consistent with other scholars' research on popular literacy and education narratives. For example, Mike Rose, in *Lives on the Boundary*, wrote about the strong belief of the veterans he worked with that "[e]ducation held the power to equalize things" (137). In addition, Janet Carey Eldred and Peter Mortensen have written about popular literacy narratives containing "culturally scripted ideas," including the "progress plot"—the belief that literacy or education is required to achieve success (513). This "progress plot" (what Kirk Branch has called the "traditional literacy narrative") is a story "in which literacy literally lifts people into a new and more productive way of living in and seeing the world" (208). When written or promoted by teachers, Branch argues, this narrative has the power to re-inscribe the "great divide" theory of literacy that assumes a large cognitive gap between those who are literate and those who are not, and that literate persons can save or aid the illiterate by teaching them.

What students' comments about education tell us, then, is that they are motivated to learn and to get their GEDs, they are motivated by their desires for self-improvement as well as bettering the lives of others. They also reveal that their motivations reflect cultural beliefs and myths that equate education with life improvement. These motivations are far from the "learning for the sake of learning" motivation at the heart of traditional views of intellectualism. They are also, however, more than the economic motivations politicians and policy makers assume drive these students and institutions. Consequently, reimagining intellectualism so it does not limit motivational forces to learning for its own sake allows us to include in its parameters the interviewees—people who have not had the material circumstances that support learning for leisure.

Views of Intelligence and Intellectualism

In addition to asking students about their interest in education and their educational experiences, I asked them how they define intelligence, what characteristics they associate with someone they consider intelligent, and whether or not they consider themselves intelligent. I asked only the first six students I interviewed how they define intellectualism because the question made them self-conscious: they did not know what I was talking about, and the confusion interrupted the flow of the interview.[4] In subsequent interviews, I asked students more questions about their and others' attitudes toward learning and education to try to uncover similar data without using the term *intellectual*. Combined, students' responses to my questions about intelligence, intellectualism, and attitudes toward learning shed additional light on their views of education and learning.

Carin's description of someone who is intelligent entails many of the characteristics that most of the students associated with an intelligent person:

> The way they carry theirself, their mannerisms, how they always have the . . . they know what they're talkin' about. They're not gullible. Pronunciation has a lot to do with it. That's what I think of an intelligent person. Not book smart, cause there's people who are very intelligent, but they don't have the book smarts . . . I don't think I'm smart in the way of higher education cause I don't have a PhD, a master, a bachelor. I don't even have a GED, so I don't view myself as smart in that area, but I do use common sense when it comes to everyday life.

Like Carin, many of the students associated intelligence with "how you carry yourself," speaking well, and common sense. In fact, these were the three most popular characteristics students associated with an intelligent person. Other characteristics students associated with being intelligent included not being gullible, being a good person, being good at what you do, having respect for yourself and others, doing the right thing, not being "ghetto," being able to understand life, and having knowledge to give to others.

Most students dissociated intelligence from book smarts, education level, and measures of academic success. For example, when I asked Wendell what it means to be intelligent, he said,

> It's not always bein' educated bookwise that will make you intelligent. You can take a college bookworm out of college and put him in the ghetto and he will be dumbfounded and vice versa. You could take an uneducated person out of the ghetto and put him in college and he'd be dumbfounded. It depends on the individual.

Carl made a similar distinction:

> A person that is intelligent is not always book smart. A person that gets straight A's may be smart at the books or ya know or the bigger picture of life and be able to analyze the bigger things in life like ya know at the blink of an eye, but when it comes to the everyday situation lifestyle, sometimes they try and analyze too much and miss the big picture. To be intelligent you don't have to be book smart, but you do have to have a feel for the world . . . it takes more to be smart than getting good grades and studyin' cause sometimes you just gotta be able to use common sense and they don't teach you stuff like that in the books.

When I asked Wendell if he considers himself intelligent he said,

> Even though I don't have a high school diploma or anything, and I'm lacking in some areas, I consider myself agewise intelligent. I'm 60 years old and I've been around for awhile, and so I know a lot about life in general . . . so I'd consider myself intelligent, not schoolwise intelligent, but yes.

Kim said she didn't know if she considers herself smart, but she considers herself intelligent: "I'm not no dummy or no fool. I got, like, common sense, but I'm not smart, smart." She continued, saying someone who is smart is someone who knows everything. That's why she doesn't consider herself smart. She says it takes her a long time to catch on to things.[5] William said he considers himself a little intelligent because, he said,

> I have some knowledge that people may not think I have even though I did not graduate from high school. Like as far as like I know some laws . . . I know about some of the economy situations that's goin' on. I worked, like, two political things. I worked the Hillary Clinton campaign and I learned about stuff through that.[6]

Carl identified as intelligent, noting his common sense and his ability to see education from multiple perspectives.

Based on their comments, students recognize that intelligence is traditionally associated with book smarts and with academic success (in the form of degrees). Yet, these students employ a different definition of intelligence, one that includes them. They define it in nonacademic terms, associating it with some of what they already possess, including common sense, life experience, and "real-world" knowledge (none of which are lauded by traditional views of intellectualism). Although they recognize that academic success increases access to things they desire, they don't equate that success with intelligence. Instead, many of them label that being "book smart."

While I did not ask many of the students about intellectualism, two of the students I asked did make some telling claims. I highlight their responses because they show that, in contrast to their views of intelligence, these two students define *intellectual* in the traditional sense, associating it with academics and high levels of education. In other words, they do not identify as intellectuals or define intellectual in a way that includes them.

Cited in the introduction to this book, Carl identified an intellectual with someone who gets his or her confidence through academic success, is an "aggressive learner," and has one perspective of school. Seeing himself as someone with multiple perspectives on education and someone who does not attain his confidence from success in school, Carl did not identify as an intellectual and seemed to adamantly not want to identify as such. When I asked Carl if there is anyone he would call an intellectual, he said yes, a friend of his who attends college. He said he considers his friend an intellectual person "because he knows everything. I don't know if he knows everything, but he thinks he knows."

Wendell is the only person who immediately said "yes" when I asked if he'd heard of the term intellectual. When I asked him what it is, he said the following:

> To me an intellectual is a bookworm. I mean they pretty much know the whole dictionary . . . or, you can try and talk to an intellectual and they'll use words to a common person instead of being able to come down to that common person's level so that they can understand what they're sayin'. They'll use words they know because they don't know how to come back down anymore. . . . I mean a big time intellectual. You don't have to be like all that to be an intellectual. Attorneys have to be an intellectual to do their job. Supervisors, bosses, CEOs, all those would be intellectuals cause they have to be.

Based on their responses, these two students ascribe to the narrow and stereotypical views of intellectualism this research challenges (high intelligence, academic success). It is interesting in this case that students espouse a definition of intellectualism aligned with the one perpetuated by the dominant culture (especially traditional academic institutions), even though it does not include them. This contradiction in Carl's and Wendell's responses (defining *intelligent* in a way that includes them while subscribing to the traditional view of intellectualism), along with other students' desire to be considered intelligent and their unfamiliarity with the term intellectual, is not surprising. These students have never been a part of a community considered intellectual and they are part of a national public repeatedly labeled anti-intellectual and ignorant. They have also been educated by public institutions that value intelligence but were not preparing them to become intellectuals in the traditional sense. In addition, their definitions accord with the larger cultural tendency to identify with and value intelligence but distance oneself from and remain skeptical of intellectualism (such as the ambivalence toward intellectualism Hofstadter documented). In this case, students are comfortable identifying as intelligent but not intellectual or book smart.

Particularly striking about Carl and Wendell's statements are their criticisms of intellectuals. While they imply intellectuals are motivated by the desire for "more freedom," confidence, and good jobs—motivations the students at the Lindberg Center share with them—Carl and Wendell consider intellectuals' views of education narrow because they only value academic education and intelligence and fail to recognize their other forms.

While the students represent a population not typically associated with intellectualism (and they even disidentify from that label themselves), their comments about education, motivations for working on a GED, and views of intelligence and intellectualism demonstrate that they have entered the writing workshops valuing education, valuing multiple forms of education, and motivated to learn—characteristics of intellectualism as this book seeks to define it. Their comments also suggest that they come to the workshops influenced by longstanding cultural beliefs that affect their ideas about education, including "the progress plot," the literacy myth, and traditional views of intellectualism. The workshop teachers and program supervisor have added that students come with much experience thinking critically about their environment but don't recognize it as such. Cate said,

> I think a majority of our students have had to be very creative problem solvers their entire lives. But I don't think they always recognize what that skill is and how to apply it in another environment that they're not sure that they're comfortable in.

A close look at the writing workshops curriculum can illuminate more fully to what extent the program builds on what students bring to the classroom, fostering students' interest in learning and providing opportunities for deliberation and critical thinking.

THE WORKSHOPS

In what follows, I describe and evaluate the activities and content of the writing workshops as I observed them and from the perspective of the teachers, students, and program administrator. My analysis challenges perceptions of basic literacy programs as necessarily "marginal to the intellectual community" (Rose, *Lives on the Boundary* 195) by demonstrating that these workshops present students with content that helps them critique social and cultural issues central to their lives and also with assignments and activities that challenge them and encourage critical thinking—characteristics central to a more inclusive and democratic view of intellectualism. I begin by describing in some detail one workshop that represents well many of the attributes of the twelve workshops I observed. I follow the description with my analysis of the intellectual import of the workshops.

It's 4:45 P.M. on an ordinary winter day and the students are settling in at the three large tables that take up most of the workshop room. Matt (the outreach consultant teaching the evening workshops) gets the two-and-a-half-hour-long workshop started by handing out a poem by Paul Laurence Dunbar[7] titled "Sympathy." A student volunteers to read the poem aloud to the class. Matt starts the discussion of the poem by asking students why they think the poem is called "Sympathy." A young man answers, "'Cause he feels for the bird." Another student adds, "'Cause the bird's caged and wants to be free." Matt then asks what the bird is doing in the poem, and a female student says, "Singing!" Matt moves the discussion forward by pointing to a passage from the poem: "It is not a carol of joy or glee, / But a prayer that he sends from his heart's deep core." Matt asks why the sound of the bird singing might not sound beautiful, and a student replies, "'Cause it's hurtin' itself." "Sure," Matt says, "the speaker is thinking about the bird beating its wings on the cage and the pain for the bird." Matt asks, then, why the author would want to write about this—about a caged bird beating its wings and crying in pain. A young man says, "'Cause the author might feel pain hisself." "Like a metaphor," another student adds.

Matt then asks the class what a metaphor is. A student says, "The pain the bird's having is the same as the pain of the author." "Right," Matt says, "like the caged bird is a metaphor for a lack of freedom." Matt points out that the author, Dunbar, was an African American poet and asks "Why might he want to use a poem to talk about a lack of freedom?" A student replies, "Maybe 'cause he was caged in." Matt pushes their reading of the poem a bit further by adding that the poem was written after the Civil War, so African Americans technically had freedom by then. The poem, he says, is an example of taking a seemingly simple image (a bird singing in a cage) and using it to show complexity.

Matt instructs the students, then, to write their own poem with the same title. He asks them to think about how they define sympathy. He tells them they can use metaphor in their poem, like Dunbar does, but they don't have to. He tells the students this activity is "to get the gears goin' . . . to get us thinkin'." In the time they have, some students write quietly, while others ask Matt questions or ask him or one of the assistants to look at and comment on their poems. After about twenty minutes, Matt collects the students' poems and promises to return them the next week, along with a group poem he will assemble containing a line or two from each student's individual poem.

Before moving on to the more formal writing work he has planned for the workshop, Matt takes a few minutes (while he's collecting their poems) to ask students what their own ideas and thoughts about writing poetry are. One student says, "It's alright. I'm not really into poetry like that. I can write raps and stuff like that." Matt asks, then, what the difference is between poetry and rap. The student says, "Rap has more umph," and another student says, "I don't think they're different. They're all about expression." After a few more comments about rap and poetry, Matt concludes by telling the students it's important to find some writing that they like to do because the more writing they do, the more their writing will improve.

Next on the agenda for this workshop is a worksheet on commas that the class completes together. Matt encourages the students to use the worksheet as a tool—something to refer back to when they have questions about how and when to use commas in their writing. Then, to prepare students for the work they will do in the second half of the workshop, Matt reviews their writing assignment from the previous workshop. During the last workshop students wrote individual letters to Barack Obama voicing two or three concerns they have and how they'd like the president to address them. They revisit the parts of the letter: a salutation, introduction, two to three body paragraphs (each dealing with one issue), and a conclusion. Matt transitions the students from the structure of the letters they wrote into the structure of the five-paragraph essay, the type of essay students must write for the GED writing exam. Just before their fifteen-minute break, Matt hands out a sample five-paragraph essay that models for students the parts and structure they need in their essays.

When students return from their short break, they are given a writing prompt and the rest of the time (about an hour) to write and revise a practice five-paragraph essay. The writing prompt this evening is, "Our opinions change. Identify an opinion you once held but that you had given up or changed. Write an essay explaining how and why the change occurred." As students write, they take turns asking for help from Matt or one of the assistants in the room. Based on the feedback they receive, they revise, develop, and rewrite their essays several times. The purpose of this time, it is clear, is individual, hands-on instruction for students, geared toward helping them with their individual writing challenges, especially as they relate to preparing them for the GED exam.

Workshop Activities

As my description of this workshop shows, the type and sequencing of learning and thinking activities used by teachers are integral to the intellectual work of the sessions. Like this one, each workshop begins with an engaging and exploratory creative activity followed by more formal writing exercises and assignments aimed at preparing students for the GED test. The creative activities introduce students to the writing and experiences of others and give them the freedom to explore and communicate (both in their writing and in class discussions) their own ideas about a variety of issues. Matt explained his use of these creative activities as a way to get students thinking critically.

In the workshop in this example, the creative activity involves reading and discussing a poem and then writing one that allows students to explore how the theme of the poem relates to their own lives and experiences. Another creative activity Matt used was having students read and discuss a funny article from the mock news source, *The Onion*.[8] He said that because he knew students were not familiar with *The Onion*, he used an article from it to introduce them to the "upper-middle class highly-educated white irony" indicative of the publication. For Matt,

> just sort of bringing the concept of irony and thinking about the kind of cultural divisions that make that kind of irony inaccessible to students at the Lindberg Center workshop is one way that they can kind of engage critically with this material.

Blanche, the teacher of the afternoon workshops, used the following creative activities: reading and discussing short writings by Malcolm X, Terry Tempest Williams, Henry Louis Gates Jr., and Alice Walker; reading and discussing poems by George Ella Lyon and Nikki Giovanni; writing individual poems or group poems; and a "picture prompt" exercise for which students looked at a painting and wrote a poem to accompany it. Though Matt didn't make clear to students that he was introducing them to *The Onion* article as a piece of "upper-middle class highly-educated white irony" and though Matt's discussion of "Sympathy" with students and some of the discussions in Blanche's class were brief, these activities still give students experience critiquing a variety of texts.

The more formal writing exercises and assignments Matt and Blanche use are also designed and sequenced to, in Matt's words, "exercise students' mental muscles." These "mental muscles" include skills like brainstorming, organizing, comparing, analyzing, describing, summarizing, revising, and storytelling. For example, in her first session of the series, Blanche used a "words, sentences, and paragraphs" activity that asked students to practice writing paragraphs in three steps, by beginning with words, then composing sentences from those words, then using those sentences as topic sentences for full paragraphs. The following week students wrote about their own experiences with literacy. In the third workshop, Blanche went over the scoring guide and checklist for the GED writing test and worked with students as they wrote five-paragraph essays. The following week students worked on outlining and then writing a five-paragraph essay with a new prompt. In the final workshop of the series, Blanche let students choose from creative writing activities and grammar/sentence-level worksheets.

In the first workshop of the six-week series, Matt asked students to write an essay about themselves and their interest in reading and writing. He introduced the assignment, saying, "For now, don't worry about writing a formal essay. Just tell a story about yourself and use lots of details." The following week he had students write the letters to President Obama I described earlier. He used this assignment to discuss with students the function of audience, style, and purpose along with the parts of a letter, giving them a bit more structure with this assignment. The next week he reviewed the structure of the letter and then tied it to the structure of the five-paragraph essay they must master for the GED test. The assignment that night was the previously mentioned five-paragraph essay about an opinion students changed and how and why the change occurred. In the fifth workshop, Matt had students write seven paragraphs in which they practiced the skills of summarizing, describing, analyzing, and comparing two famous paintings.[9] During the final workshop, students worked again on writing the formal five-paragraph essay, this time about specific ways the economy is affecting the students (a topic students communally created). This combination and sequencing of assignments exercised students' "mental muscles"—engaging them in critical thinking.

When I asked students about the workshops, their comments were overwhelmingly positive. A characteristic of the workshops students found most helpful was the "breaking down" of the material into smaller pieces that they can understand (something many of them said they didn't get in elementary or high school). William said,

> I like how it gets broke down to where I can understand it better. In high school they just told us to write an essay and that was it. They didn't give you the chance to break it down and understand.

Breaking the material down for students makes it more accessible, useful, and perhaps more interesting to them. It also can help them engage with the material in ways they weren't able to in other educational contexts.

When I asked students about the creative activities, a majority of the students said they enjoy the creative writing, though they differed on seeing a connection between the creative and more formal writing. For example, Wendell said, "I can't see no purpose in it rather than just getting the students relaxed and comfortable and ready for the next phase." In contrast, LaShonda saw a direct connection:

> [The creative activities] work on me because I got loosened up, because before I wasn't used to writin' for a long time, so I had to get back into the writin' and usin' my imagination. [These activities] help you stimulate your imagination and try to get you to thinking, ya know what I'm sayin' cause you're gonna have to open up your mind to get through that essay because you're gonna have to write five paragraphs.

Another student spoke about the creative writing activities allowing her to break through the stress on her mind when she arrives at workshop: "I like them cause I think it releases a lot that you have on your mind." Kim described how an activity they did that afternoon prompted her to write about how she feels like she's living in a box because of all the things she has to do for her mother and her girls when she leaves workshop. While comments like Wendell's demonstrate how students don't necessarily see the skill-level connection between the two types of writing, the sequencing of these activities is designed to encourage students to apply and transfer the critical thinking they more easily engage in for the creative activities to the more structured writing of the five-paragraph essay.

In addition to using the creative activities to get students "warmed up" for the more formal writing, Matt said he attempts to connect the two activities by helping students recognize these writing activities as different rhetorical situations. In one situation, students are being asked to respond to and critically analyze a poem; in another they're taking a test. Matt says he talks to students about the "machinery" surrounding them in the different situations and how to respond appropriately in each. What he's trying to do, he says, is develop in the students "a sort of switch [they] can flip" when they go into the test-taking situation.

> If you get them to that sort of intellectual place where they're able to critically analyze the writing situation they're being put in for the purpose of this exam, then you're not just putting them through a kind of GED writing boot camp; you're actually stressing critical analysis even if you're having them produce writing [for the test] that is not very critical or analytical.

Matt's assistant Megan compared the thinking that the workshop activities required with the thinking required of college students:

> The ways in which [the Lindberg Center students] are trying to stretch their minds to perform a task, to learn a skill or a skill set, to develop strategies, to obtain a certain result—to pass the GED—is just the same as me trying to pass a theory class at [the university].

She stressed that even though students have to submit to the five-paragraph-essay style and structure, that "doesn't eliminate critical thinking." In other words, the goal of preparing students to write a five-paragraph essay for the GED exam does not mean the workshops cannot foster and support intellectualism.

Workshop Content

In addition to teaching students to be critically aware of different writing situations and preparing them to write well in those different situations, both workshop teachers bring in content that is culturally relevant and thought provoking. Cate said in her interview that while the goal of the workshops is really to help students "build concrete skills in order to pass the writing part of the GED test," every outreach consultant who has taught the workshops has made an effort to meet this goal with a curriculum that is creative and contemporary, "getting students to think about the world around them." In this way, too, workshop instructors foster students' intellectual engagement.

Because a majority of the students are African Americans from low-income or working-class backgrounds, both teachers often use the writings of authors (often African American themselves) writing about issues relevant to race and class. For example, Henry Louis Gates's "In the Kitchen" is an essay about the spot of kinky hair at the base of a black person's neck ("the kitchen") that was the one part of the body that undeniably "resisted assimilation" into white culture. Alice Walker's "The Place Where I Was Born" is about having to leave her home because of racist oppression and economic impoverishment. Malcolm X's "Prison Studies" explores his struggle to learn to read and the power he felt when he did. In her poem "Where I'm From," George Ella Lyon paints a picture of the type of life and family she came from through details like "the dirt under the back porch" and "fried corn and strong coffee." And Paul Dunbar's "Sympathy" explores the feeling of being caged in. Having students read and write about experiences specific to their lives, like race and class, gives students the opportunity to explore and critically consider these issues.

While the instructors designed some of the more formal writing prompts to be particularly relevant to students' lives (for example, how the economy affects them and what President Obama can change for them), many of the prompts they used are actual GED essay exam prompts. These topics include the following: "Explain why you do or do not vote," "What are the essential characteristics of a good parent?," and "Name someone you consider to be a modern hero or heroine. Explain why." While students weren't always excited to write about these topics, the teachers encouraged them to see the prompts as the opportunity to write about their own personal opinions and experiences related to the topic.

What my analysis of the activities and content used in the GED-preparation workshops indicates is that despite the restrictive and formulaic nature of the five-paragraph essay students must learn for the GED test, the workshops exercise students' "mental muscles" and support their exploration of ideas. In this context, writing becomes a tool both for communicating to an audience (in the test situation), and a tool for exploring and sharing ideas. In these ways, the workshops not only satisfy students' incoming general interest in learning and help them work toward their goal of getting their GED but they also foster students' critical thinking and engagement with ideas—characteristics of a broader, more inclusive definition of intellectualism.

BASIC LITERACY EDUCATION AND INTELLECTUALISM

An analysis of the Lindberg Center's writing workshops and participants helps illuminate the complex relationship between basic literacy education and intellectualism. On one hand, the literacy activities used in the workshops can help foster intellectualism by serving as tools for critical thinking and for the expression, development, and communication of ideas. On the other hand, because traditional views of intellectualism use literacy practices and abilities (literacy versus illiteracy, reading highbrow versus lowbrow texts, strong literacy skills versus weak literacy skills) to delineate the intellectual from the nonintellectual, the literacy activities at the center of the writing workshop curriculum are assumed to be nonintellectual.

For example, the five-paragraph essay (the product students are ultimately being taught to write for the GED exam) has typically been seen as rigid, stifling, and oversimplified, particularly by rhetoric and composition scholars. In addition, though the texts students are reading in the workshops are also taught in university classrooms, because the readings are short and are not read and analyzed through an academic lens such as literary theory, this "reading practice" is not viewed by all academics as intellectual. For instance, because the discussion of Dunbar's poem "Sympathy" in Matt's workshop centered on students' opinions and experiences, some scholars would not consider it an "intellectual activity." However, a discussion of the same poem in a graduate or undergraduate class that was lengthier and included the application of literary theory to the text may be considered intellectual by those same critics.

Another way to better understand the relationship between basic literacy education and intellectualism is to look more closely at the beliefs the Lindberg Center students brought with them to the program, the assumptions about literacy implicit in the center's curriculum, and how the curriculum's assumptions about literacy seem to have affected students' thinking about literacy.

While I didn't ask students specifically to discuss their beliefs about literacy prior to their participation in the writing workshops, their responses to questions about whether or not they used to read or write much outside of school, what types of reading and writing they did (if any) outside of school, and whether or not they enjoyed reading and writing reveal that most students started the program enjoying reading (but not doing much of it on their own) and not enjoying writing. LaShonda was unique among her peers in that she had always loved to read and even prior to participating in the program she used writing to help her deal with things: "I used to write to pass everything I was going through. It was wonderful for me—a healing process." William admitted that as a youth minister (something he was doing before he started the program) he has spent a good amount of time outside of class reading the Bible and writing sermons. He also talked about spending time writing grant proposals for people he knows who are trying to get help starting their own businesses. Because these literacy activities are being performed outside the context of a university classroom, and because students in a remedial education program are assumed to be marginal to the intellectual community, traditional views of intellectualism would not include these literacy activities under the rubric of intellectualism.

If we interpret students' belief that education increases access to things and leads to a better life as encompassing literacy skills, then we can assume they began the program also indirectly associating literacy with access and a better life. Additionally, their tendency to tie education to self-respect and adequacy can be read as a belief that literacy, too, leads to self-respect and adequacy. Interestingly, though, because most students did not associate intelligence with "book smarts," this could be read as not associating intelligence with literacy. Again, their weak literacy skills, then, would not prohibit them from defining themselves as intelligent. In contrast, the tendency of students to disassociate "book smarts" from "common sense," and to not identify as "book smart," along with a few students' association of "book smarts" and "bookworm" with "intellectual" demonstrates further that students do not see themselves as literate or highly literate persons. Overall, then, students appear to have started the program associating literacy with "book smarts" and academic learning, skills they disassociate themselves from.

The assumptions about literacy implicit in the center's curriculum (based on the curriculum and on the instructors' comments to me during the interviews) include the following: reading and writing can stimulate student thinking; creative writing and reading activities in particular "get [students] thinking" and thinking critically; the more writing students do, the more their writing will improve; the five-paragraph essay the GED exam requires is more stifling, formulaic, and less creative than other types of writing; revision is important; writing models can help students improve their writing; the types of "mental muscles" the more formal writing exercises and assignments exercise include brainstorming, organizing, comparing, describing, summarizing, and analyzing. As an observer of the workshops for the past three years (with a variety of workshop instructors), Cate said this about the opportunities for critical thinking the workshops provide: "Well, I think writing by nature is something you have to create, something you can't just regurgitate." Her comment reiterates the assumption that while the five-paragraph essay can be formulaic and stifling, students still must generate ideas and think about how to execute them clearly when writing the essays.

To what extent have the assumptions about literacy embedded in the center's curriculum transferred to (or affected) students' own thinking about literacy? Based on students' comments, some of them agree with the belief that the more you write the better your writing gets, and some agree that creative writing activities can improve their writing by helping to relax them and get their minds flowing. When I asked her about how the creative writing activities help with the GED exam, Kim answered, "I figure if you keep on writin', eventually you're gonna get the point of how to write an essay." Cited earlier, while Wendall said he thought the only connection between the creative writing activities and the more formal GED test prep was to relax students, LaShonda and Kim both mentioned they did see the connection. In LaShonda's words, "They work on me cause I get loosened up." In other words, some of the students buy into the center's message that reading and writing activities can improve thinking skills as well as reading and writing skills.

Student comments didn't reveal to me whether or not the other assumptions about literacy implicit in the center's curriculum affected their thinking about literacy. For example, I'm not sure if students came away seeing the five-paragraph essay as a stifling or less critical form of writing. For sure, they sounded like they had more fun writing the creative pieces, but despite instructors' biases about the five-paragraph essay, students are committed to mastering it because they know it's what is valued on the GED exam. They also seemed to feel more successful as students and as writers when they saw improvements in their writing of the five-paragraph essay, as opposed to the creative texts.

To what extent the curriculum has affected students' thinking about literacy is one thing. The extent to which it has affected their literacy practices is another. Based on student comments, these workshops have, for some students, fostered (or rekindled) an interest and engagement in literacy activities. For instance, Teresa said she never was much of a writer, but since she's been at the Lindberg Center, she's been getting more into it. "Cause I felt like I was a failure, like I don't know nothing about writing, but when I got here, it changed everything." In this way, participation in the workshops raised Teresa's confidence as a writer, which made her want to do more writing. Carl said he's always read, but he's been starting to write more since coming back to school: "Goin' back to school and getting my mind goin', it's getting me to a place where I do more writin'." Jerome said, "By me bein' here I have a little more passion for like pickin' up a book. Now I'll actually open it and go through it, so I've come a long way." And Dina said,

> A lot of times when I go home, like if I feel depressed or I don't have anything to do or am tired of the television, I go get some notebook paper and pen and I can just be sitting and writing . . . I wrote a moon poem so well to where I was like What is this? It just came straight outta me. I was surprised. And it all came from the Lindberg Center because I hadn't wrote in so long.

Other students admitted, however, that while their participation in the program may make them want to do more reading and writing, in practice they don't actually do more. For instance, when I asked Wendell if he thinks his reading and writing practices have changed since starting the program, he replied, "Ah, thus far, no. I mean I'm doin' it, but I'm only doin' it here."

Despite these positive effects the Lindberg Center has had on students' beliefs about literacy and literacy practices, it is important to note that the workshops to some extent reinforce beliefs in the literacy "progress plot" myths. While the instructors engage students in thinking critically about some of the social and cultural forces that affect many of the students, because these discussions are not situated in relation to students' education experiences or their attitudes toward literacy and education, the center's message that getting a GED brings down barriers supports the myths that literacy and education necessarily create access—something all of the interviewees were motivated by. In addition, because the work students do is not framed by the center or the instructors as intellectual work, the workshops perpetuate (even if passively) critics' and students' beliefs that the work they're doing does not fall under the rubric of intellectualism. Reimagining intellectualism as this book proposes would allow us to see education from, as Carl would say, "multiple perspectives" and help us recognize the intellectual import of these twenty-first-century literacy workshops. If, additionally, workshop instructors explicitly framed the work in the classroom as intellectual in nature, students could begin to identify as participants in an intellectual community.

The "Great Divide"

The tendency to tie low or basic literacy skills to low levels of intelligence (and consequently to a lack of intellectualism) has been in practice for a long time and has been called by scholars the "great divide" theory of literacy. The "great divide" theory postulates that literacy contributes to "higher-order" thinking and cognitive skills that divides preliterate cultures and societies from literate ones (Scribner and Cole). Literacy scholar Brian Street has explained the theory as follows:

> For individuals this is taken to mean that ways of thinking, cognitive abilities, facility in logic, abstraction and higher order mental operations are all integrally related to the achievement of literacy: the corollary is that "illiterates" are presumed to lack all of these qualities, to be able to think less abstractly, to be more embedded, less critical, less able to reflect upon the nature of the language they use or the sources of their political oppression. (21)

This view that associates literacy struggles with ignorance (Street 207) has been used in critiques of basic writers. The assumption, as Mike Rose has described, is that "poor writers can't form abstractions; they are incapable of analysis; they perceive the world as an undifferentiated whole; the speech patterns they've acquired in their communities seriously limit their critical capacity" ("Narrowing" 268).

Rhetoric and composition scholars have been challenging the notion that basic writing and basic writers are "marginal to the intellectual community" for over fifty years now. In her notable research, Mina Shaughnessy claimed that basic writing students "write the way they do, not because they are slow or non-verbal, indifferent to or incapable of academic excellence, but because they are beginners and must, like all beginners, learn by making mistakes" (5). Similarly, Marcia Dickson argued that basic writing students are "seldom inherently less intelligent or poorer critical thinkers than their better-trained peers" (vii), and Laura Gray-Rosendale illustrated the complexity of basic writing students' thinking about their lives by looking at the skills they do possess, rather than the skills they lack.

Other scholars have called for basic writing pedagogies that would challenge and empower students. Deborah Mutnick called for a writing pedagogy that would grant to basic writing students the agency and authority they are typically denied. David Bartholomae and Anthony Petrosky promoted and designed a basic writing curriculum not based on grammar exercises and drills, but rather based on engaging students with challenging reading and writing assignments. And Mike Rose has argued,

> We must be vigilant that the systems of intellect we develop or adapt do not ground our students' difficulties in sweeping, essentially one-dimensional perceptual, neurophysiological, psychological, or linguistic processes, systems that drive broad cognitive wedges between those who do well in our schools and those who don't. ("Narrowing the Mind" 297)

Despite research challenging the "great divide" theory of literacy, the most recent scholarship on basic writing reveals a troublesome trend in higher education: institutions marginalizing basic writing—seeing it as a threat to or evidence of a lack of "excellence" or intellectual prestige. Evidence shows that in an effort to maintain or gain prestige, four-year colleges have been diminishing or eliminating basic writing programs (Greene and McAlexander 1). For example, known as a leader in basic writing scholarship and pedagogy since its open admissions policy and the work of Shaughnessy and others in the 1970s, the City University of New York eliminated basic writing from its senior colleges in 1999, forcing students to seek out remediation from its community colleges. With such actions, legislators and administrators are relegating remediation to the institutions given the least amount of financial resources (Rose, *Back to School* 127). While some elite schools are maintaining their basic writing programs, they have been said to be using them to keep up the "perception" that they are committed to democratic access (Stanley). Despite these efforts to marginalize basic writing, scholars foresee a future with increased need for such remedial programs (Otte and Mlynarczyk), though what institutions will offer them, who gets defined as a basic writer, how the courses get taught, and how they are perceived by institutions themselves is difficult to predict.

Combined, views like the "great divide" theory and the assumption that intellectualism is tied to high levels of literacy and engagement with high-brow literature and texts at elite institutions relegate adult basic literacy education programs like the writing workshops at the Lindberg Center to nonintellectual learning environments. Consequently, adult learners like Carl, Teresa, Kim, and Wendell cannot recognize themselves as participants in an intellectual community. As Kirk Branch noted in his research, "While students at all levels of education have the potential to be singled out as deficient or underskilled, in adult literacy education, all of them are labeled basic, deficient, underskilled" (221). Such views most likely contribute to students' connecting their GED with self-respect, feeling they will be viewed as inadequate or deficient until they no longer need basic education. Because the definition of intellectualism proposed by this book focuses on an interest in, appreciation for, and engagement with knowledge, learning, deliberation, critical thinking, and inquiry irrespective of the particular knowledge, texts, or institutions a person engages with, it challenges the "great divide" view, and instead opens the door for the work being done at the Lindberg Center to be recognized as intellectual.

Because traditional views of intellectualism are based on problematic dichotomies that assume basic literacy education cannot be intellectual, nontraditional sites of learning like the Lindberg Center's GED writing workshops are overlooked in considerations of American intellectualism. Building on the work of scholars who challenge the belief that basic writers are cognitively deficient, this research challenges the assumption that adults participating in a GED program—and the program itself—cannot be intellectual. As this examination reveals, students participating in the workshops are motivated, interested learners whose life experiences have made them critical thinkers about their environment. The workshops foster students' interest in learning and critical engagement through culturally relevant content and purposefully designed and sequenced assignments and activities. Literacy practices are central to the workshop curriculum, and consequently are integral to the workshops' sponsoring of intellectualism.

Chapter 5 links my examinations of the intellectual contributions of American lyceums, labor colleges, and writing workshops at the Lindberg Center. Together, these three case studies challenge accepted views of intellectualism that privilege certain types of knowledge, motivations for learning, educational activities, and locations of learning. They also demonstrate the value of redefining intellectualism so it recognizes the broad spectrum of ways of thinking and engaging the mind Americans participate in within nonelite, nontraditional learning environments. Connecting my interpretations of these sites expands our understanding of intellectualism in the United States over time and place and the forces that shape our views of learning and its value.

chapter five

MAKING CONNECTIONS

The Theory and Practice of Intellectualism in the United States

REVISITING THE THREE EDUCATIONAL SPACES in U.S. history in the last three chapters makes clear that while they were started for different purposes, targeted different audiences, and disseminated different information at varied times and places, they share a mission to make education accessible to a population whose formal education has been limited by material circumstances. They also share a pool of participants who partake voluntarily and are eager to learn, and a "curriculum" that combines the dissemination of useful (sometimes basic) knowledge with learning and literacy activities that encourage critical thinking, deliberation, and inquiry. Unfortunately, because limited views of intellectualism have historically privileged the knowledge, learning sites, and educational experiences of the cultural elite, the contributions these institutions have made to American intellectualism have been discounted or overlooked by scholars, cultural critics, and many Americans.

At a time when narrow, exclusionary views of intellectualism are exacerbated by a ubiquitous rhetoric of anti-intellectualism and ignorance that informs and shapes contemporary debates about education, literacy, and learning, it is important that rhetoric, composition, and literacy studies scholars join the conversation and aid in reimagining intellectualism in the twenty-first century. What these past three chapters have sought to show are the benefits of reimagining intellectualism as an interest in, appreciation for, and engagement with learning, knowledge, deliberation, critical thinking, and inquiry. Not only does this view better reflect the aspirations of educational institutions in this country but it also democratizes the term so that it can counter the rhetoric of anti-intellectualism and ignorance, disrupt problematic educational hierarchies, and challenge variants of the literacy myth and "great divide" theory that relegate some literacy practices intellectual and others nonintellectual. Consequently, it helps us to recognize and celebrate a broad range of intellectual activities and educational institutions that represent well adult public education in the United States over time and place.

THE RHETORIC OF ANTI-INTELLECTUALISM AND IGNORANCE

As the survey of literature in chapter 1 made clear, the calls of crisis and decline in U.S. literacy and learning from the 1960s to the present promote a popular image of Americans (and American youth in particular) as anti-intellectual consumers of mind-numbing media and job-oriented degrees from colleges that fail in their intellectual mission. This rhetoric discourages the American public—and especially our students—from seeing themselves as participants in an intellectual community. It also sends the message that the United States is void of intellectuals and intellectualism outside its elite universities and that the future of American intellectualism is dependent on academics functioning as "public intellectuals" who relay knowledge to the masses.

The preceding analysis of literacy and learning at nontraditional sites of adult public education in the United States over time and place works to counter this influential rhetoric by demonstrating that if we reimagine intellectualism as an interest in, appreciation for, and engagement with learning, knowledge, deliberation, critical thinking, and inquiry, then we can recognize that Americans *have engaged* and *do engage* in valuable intellectual work. In the nineteenth century, we see evidence that the American lyceum made accessible to many Americans a variety of useful knowledge which likely would have fostered a thirst for more knowledge among participants and sent the message that knowledge and education are valuable. In some of its forms, the lyceum encouraged inquiry and deliberation through discussion, debate, and dialogue.

In the twentieth century the activism-focused curriculum at Brookwood Labor College situated students' knowledge of and experience with the labor movement in the context of historical, social, political, and economic issues, aiding them in thinking more deeply and more critically about labor issues of the time. It also taught them reading, writing, and speaking skills designed to aid them in their activist work. Because of the activist focus of the school, it not only inspired participants to be active, analytical learners themselves but it motivated them to educate others through their activist work. And in the twenty-first century the Lindberg Center's GED writing workshops built on students' interest in education and motivation to learn with a curriculum and pedagogy that encouraged students to see literacy as a tool for thinking more deeply and more critically and for communicating their ideas to others, both creatively and in a more structured form.

Together these images of the American public (particularly those unable to access more elite forms of education) as active, analytical learners contradict the popular and profitable image of Americans as couch-potato buffoons more interested in distracting themselves with media than in educating themselves or others. Instead, we see an audience listening to a lecture on slavery, townspeople debating the rights of women at a meeting, a family reading about geology, laborers writing and performing for others plays that depict the terrible conditions of workers, students discussing the ways in which the program they are participating in *is* and *is not* meeting its goals, labor movement participants returning to their work understanding more fully the larger issues influencing that work, African American adults with low literacy levels reading and writing about issues of race and class, and low-income students writing poems and five-paragraph essays in which they express their own ideas and learn to develop them more fully. Recognizing these images as depictions of American intellectualism is far more democratic and meaningful than the widespread and traditional image of an intellectual as a white college professor with glasses, a chalkboard, and a stack of books.

EDUCATIONAL HIERARCHIES

The preceding three case studies demonstrate clearly that traditional views of intellectualism are based on and perpetuate problematic educational hierarchies, including hierarchies of knowledge, of the purpose of education, of literacy and learning practices, of audience, and of institutional status. They also teach us that reimagining intellectualism in a more meaningful and inclusive way can aid in challenging and disrupting these educational hierarchies.

In the case of lyceums, the knowledge disseminated was labeled "useful"—knowledge that could be put to practical uses by the audience. Though what knowledge was considered useful varied greatly, it was all still viewed as having a practical application or outcome. At Brookwood, the knowledge provided was divided between "tool" and "informational" courses, a blend of hands-on application courses and courses providing the information believed to be needed to empower students in their activist work for the labor movement. The knowledge sought at the Lindberg Center was basic literacy—more specifically, the ability to write a five-paragraph essay in response to a GED writing prompt. While the knowledge disseminated by the instructors included but also exceeded this practical knowledge, variants of the literacy myth and the "great divide" theory of literacy that some subscribe to categorize this basic literacy knowledge nonintellectual. According to traditional views of intellectualism, intellectuals seek and acquire highbrow knowledge—the type of knowledge seen as dichotomous to the type disseminated by these institutions. As a result, these institutions—and their participants—have been overlooked in considerations of American intellectualism, in part, because of the hierarchy of knowledge propagated by traditional views of intellectualism.

Because "learning for its own sake" has been the assumed motivation for education for intellectuals, the practical purposes and motivations underlying these institutions has also positioned them outside the rubric of traditional views of intellectualism. Based on the nineteenth-century and Holbrook's use of the term "intellectual," the intellectual mission of the lyceums was to spread knowledge, understanding, and reason among the public for practical uses. The stated purpose of labor colleges was to educate workers to be successful leaders and activists for the labor movement. It was *not*, as an author in a 1923 issue of the *Brookwood Review* said, "education just for education's sake, leading nowhere save to individual advancement" (1). At the Lindberg Center, the purpose of education for the students was specifically to help them get their GEDs, but also more generally (as students' comments indicate), for overall life improvement.

For lyceums, the primary methods used to educate the public were lectures, meetings, and periodicals. Labor colleges used some traditional classroom learning activities, but they also utilized hands-on experiential education methods like having students participate in and perform labor journalism, labor drama, and other activist work. At the Lindberg Center, a variety of reading, writing, and thinking activities were used by instructors, among them instruction in composing the traditional five-paragraph essay. These activities are not the type of educational methods associated with the learning practices indicative of intellectuals studying highbrow ideas at prestigious institutions of higher education, and consequently are not associated with American intellectualism.

A stated attribute for each of the three institutions was open access to those who needed or desired the education being offered. As my reexamination of the sites shows, while each site provided access to those whose material circumstances excluded them from other forms of education, there were still limits to who was able to attend or participate. However, because educational institutions deemed intellectual are seen as accessible only to the intellectual and cultural elite, institutions targeted at nonelite or unprivileged populations—or open to "all"—are dismissed in discussions of intellectualism based on their intended audience. Similarly, the assumption has been that elite institutions of higher education such as Ivy League and other prestigious colleges are the arbiters of intellectualism, and adult education programs like these three are vocational or recreational (in other words, not intellectual).

Mike Rose helps us understand this institutional divide when he traces the history of the split between academic and vocational education. According to Rose, the 1917 Smith-Hughes Act gave national legitimacy to the vocational education movement by mandating separate governing boards, funding sources, and instructional programs for vocational schools. The result was the institutionalizing of cultural and educational biases about intelligence. Because those who work with their hands are assumed to be less intelligent than those who work with their minds, the institutions that prepare students for those respective jobs are judged similarly. In other words, academic programs cultivate the mind, while vocational programs prepare students for work ("Intelligence, Knowledge"). For this reason also, educational institutions like lyceums, Brookwood Labor College, and the Lindberg Center are not recognized as intellectual spaces.

Among the consequences of these educational hierarchies is that they privilege and place more cultural and economic value on the knowledge, learning sites, and educational experiences of the cultural elite. This view unfairly—and consequentially—separates kinds of knowledge and the institutions associated with them, leading to assumptions that any learning related to work or taking place in a vocational setting is absent intellectual possibilities. Based on these assumptions, institutions deemed "vocational" are not expected to—and sometimes fail to—cultivate the intellectual development of participants (Rose, *Back to School* 78–79).

We see evidence in each case study examined here that these views affect not only how others consider nonelite learners and sites of learning but also how the participants themselves subscribe to the educational hierarchies that devalue their work and contributions. For example, in his 1830 lyceum speech, Timothy Walker made clear that the work of the lyceum was to spread "useful knowledge," "practical information," and "common sense," and not to spread "brilliancy," "wit," and "sparkling genius." A similar distinction was heard in the voices of the Lindberg Center students. Connecting intelligence to common sense and having knowledge and disassociating it from book smarts and academic success, the Lindberg students labeled themselves intelligent and wanted to be seen as intelligent. Associating intellectualism with academic success, with knowing everything, and with a limited view of education, they did not identify as intellectuals, nor did they want to be seen as intellectuals. Evidence of a similar division was found at Brookwood Labor College when, in the *Twelfth Anniversary Review* of the school, one contributor wrote that at Brookwood, "education is not confined to 'book larnin'" and that the most valuable education at the school comes "out of the exchange of experiences and ideas" between workers (10). Such comments indicate some participants at each of these institutions subscribe to the hierarchies promoted by traditional views of intellectualism. In other words, the hierarchies promoted by narrow views of intellectualism can affect Americans' views of education and intellectualism, making intellectualism seem unattainable or undesirable to those who aren't members of the cultural elite.

In addition to exposing the educational hierarchies resulting from narrow notions of intellectualism, the preceding case studies also teach us that reimagining intellectualism in a more meaningful and inclusive way can aid in challenging and disrupting these educational hierarchies. Defining intellectualism as an interest in, appreciation for, and engagement with learning, knowledge, deliberation, critical thinking, and inquiry removes the hierarchical criteria associated with those with the material circumstances and access to more privileged forms of education. Because it is focused on attitudes toward and participation in learning, rather than on a particular type of knowledge, text, educational method, audience, or institution, it allows us to recognize that intellectualism can be grounded in the acquisition of useful knowledge for practical purposes, experiential and activist learning, basic literacy education, and vocational, recreational, and adult education. This definition recognizes a larger spectrum of attitudes and ideas about learning, along with a wider range of intellectual spaces and activities. As Carl at the Lindberg Center would say, it views education from multiple perspectives.

THE LITERACY MYTH AND THE "GREAT DIVIDE"

My review of traditional views of intellectualism suggests further that the hierarchies they impose promote "powerful variants" of the literacy myth and the "great divide" theory of literacy, sending the message that certain literacy practices necessarily lead to "cognitive advancement" and intellectual development. More specifically, intellectualism has long been associated with highbrow literature and texts, and with literacy practices viewed as serving the purpose of learning for learning's sake (and not learning for practical or useful purposes). For instance, claims by the National Endowment for the Arts that a decline in literary reading produces a nation of ill-informed, passive thinkers implies that intellectualism results from reading novels, short stories, plays, or poetry. Allan Bloom's insistence that students at elite universities must read the Great Books (and must read them in a particular way) to be intellectual and E. D. Hirsch Jr.'s assertion that children must read "content-rich" books (defined as "the classics") make a similar claim. Additionally, the assumption that digital literacy practices (in other words, reading and writing online) don't incite deep reading and thinking (Carr), disrupt "irreplaceable forms of focused attention and contemplation that make complex communication and insights possible" (NEA), and are not "full-fledged intellectual practices" (Bauerlein) overshadows the possible and plentiful ways in which digital literacy practices can and do foster intellectual development. Further, the test- and consumer-driven climate of contemporary education promotes for the average student those literacy practices that produce good test takers and good workers.

The definition of intellectualism proposed here, along with my reexamination of these educational spaces and activities, work to disassociate intellectualism from a hierarchy of literacy practices. Collectively, the three case studies demonstrate that while literacy activities can be tools for fostering intellectualism, they do not by themselves lead to "cognitive advancement" or intellectual development. Instead, they demonstrate that a number of variables can affect the development of critical thinking and a desire to learn. For example, the lyceum nurtured the desire to learn by making knowledge accessible through lectures, discussion, and periodicals and sending the message that education is important. Brookwood Labor College fostered critical thinking by having students apply what they were learning in their informational courses to activist work, including producing plays, journalism, and informational materials designed to expose the issues faced by American laborers of the time. And the Lindberg Center workshops facilitated independent thinking through activities like writing letters to Obama expressing concerns about life in America and reading and discussing texts tackling social and economic issues many of the students face. As these examples show, literacy practices not valued by narrow, exclusionary definitions of intellectualism can and do play an important role in fostering intellectualism. They do not, however, by themselves ensure cognitive or intellectual advancement.

IDENTITY, STATUS, AND PROFESSIONALIZATION

The hierarchical views of education and literacy promoted and supported by narrow notions of intellectualism are at the center of some of our field's issues with identity, status, and professionalization. Considered by some in academe a "service" discipline because of its connection to courses like developmental and first-year writing, the field has been deemed by some intellectually inferior—or intellectually marginal—within English studies or within the academy at large. For others, the issue is an emphasis on teaching versus theory (or the theory-practice divide). Another hierarchical dichotomy within the academy, the theory-practice debate equates theory with highbrow, intellectual work and associates teaching with practice and less or nonintellectual work.

This debate has played out within the field's own discussions of status, professionalization, and identity. It has been called "composition's theory wars." For some, the privileging of practice over theory is anti-intellectual. This view was espoused a quarter of a century ago by Louise Wetherbee Phelps: "Deep in the disciplinary unconscious runs a strong undercurrent of anti-intellectual feeling that resists the dominance of theory in every institutional context of the field" (Phelps, qtd. in Olson 24). More recently, Lance Svehla pointed out the tendency within composition to label "anti-intellectual" those who insist that theory must be conducted in relation to and applied to teaching practices. In his history of composition studies, Joseph Harris cautioned the field against compromising its ties to teaching (or practice) in order to gain professionalization in academia because, in his words, its ties to teaching are "what give so much work in the field its political and intellectual edge" (xi). Others have complained that it is their focus on theory over practice that has led to their feeling marginalized within the field. For example, in a 2003 article on "The New Theory Wars," Lynn Worsham was quoted as saying that "for the past thirty years, people in the field have tried to define [composition studies] as an intellectual discipline, not a service component of the university. But now it seems like people are embracing it as a service component" (McLemee).

Demonstrating the centrality of this issue within the field, in 2002 a book titled *Rhetoric and Composition as Intellectual Work* was dedicated to showcasing the variety of intellectual work being done in the field. Editor Gary A. Olson said the book was a response to the hegemonic struggles the discipline has faced, particularly in relation to literary study (30). Lisa Ede followed this book with her own in which she drew on her personal experience as literary scholar and then rhetoric and composition scholar to demonstrate and question composition's troubled "location" in the academy. She argued that the field needs to reframe the theory-practice dichotomy (and tendency to privilege theory) as a practice-practice dichotomy, viewing theory and practice side by side and as equal but different forms of practice (*Situating Composition*).

Recent discussions of the field's intellectual status and contributions have centered on particular subfields of rhetoric and composition and on the division of labor within English departments. For example, Stuart A. Selber noted that the subfield of technical communication has been characterized by some as a "service discipline, an anti-intellectual field, or a corporate enterprise" (264). The intellectual heft of the digital media subfield has also been questioned by some. As Palmeri noted in his history of multimodal writing pedagogy, while some in the field assume that the intellectual benefits of digital media composing are obvious, others believe strongly that it stifles students' critical thinking and development. Additionally, the tendency to assume that basic writers and basic writing are nonintellectual has led to assumptions that the subfield of developmental writing is also intellectually marginal (Rose, *Lives on the Boundary* 195). In a recent *College English* forum discussing contingent labor and identity in the field, one of the contributors wrote of her experience that "teaching is . . . regarded as hard work performed by the staff, the amorphous mass, but not as intellectual production" (Bilia et al. 387). In fact, the field's increasing connection to contingent labor serves to distance it further from the intellectual work associated with full-time tenured and tenure-track faculty.

Couple this disciplinary struggle with what many see as the marginalization of the humanities within academia and additionally with growing sentiments that higher education's relevance (economically and intellectually) is rapidly diminishing and it becomes clear that rhetoric, composition, and literacy studies scholars need to participate in the larger (public and academic) conversations about intellectualism and anti-intellectualism in the United States. If we do not participate in challenging and reimagining traditional views of intellectualism that categorize some of our research and teaching practices, some of our subfields, and at times our entire field as intellectually marginal, then we risk personal and professional irrelevance. Also at stake are the attitudes and actions of many of our students. Positioned by society and academia as anti-intellectual consumers of mind-numbing media, students do not value their literacy and learning experiences or expect to or hope to ever contribute to American intellectualism.

As a field, we can enter this important conversation through our scholarship, as this book attempts to. We can also participate through our role as teachers by engaging our students in examinations of these issues and the consequences they have for students and American culture writ large. We can also work to equip students to navigate their literacy and learning empowered by the knowledge that narrow notions of intellectualism do not have to define them, their views, or their choices. In the next and final chapter, I highlight two projects I have used with my own students to begin this important work. I conclude the book with a chapter focused on teaching (rather than with this chapter) because it shows how our students are affected by public and academic rhetoric about intellectualism and anti-intellectualism, because it demonstrates what students and the field can learn from analyzing such rhetoric, and because it showcases students' intellectual contributions.

chapter six

INTO THE CLASSROOM

Pedagogical Approaches to the Rhetoric of Intellectualism and Anti-intellectualism

FOR THE PAST TEN YEARS, to engage my first-year composition students in the important work of thinking and writing critically about the messages concerning education and intellectualism that surround them, I have been introducing them to the prominent voices—both academic and popular—sending these messages. I have also been aiding them in examining the context, rhetorical strategies, and potential consequences of such messages. With the goals of teaching students how to think critically about the rhetoric that surrounds them and also how to effectively and thoughtfully employ rhetorical strategies in their own communication of ideas, the first-year composition course has seemed an appropriate place to encourage students to analyze and respond to this rhetoric. It is important to engage students in a study of the rhetoric of intellectualism and anti-intellectualism in the United States not only because it shapes education reform, public policy, and public ideas about literacy and learning but also because it influences students' own attitudes, experiences, and actions. In addition, it is important for us to employ a pedagogical approach that encourages and empowers students to become critical, active participants in these academic and public conversations because (as the survey in chapter 1 makes clear) students' voices are not currently present in these discussions.

In this chapter, I discuss two examples of my work engaging undergraduates in a critical analysis of the rhetoric of intellectualism and anti-intellectualism in the United States. I describe the assignments and discern both what students learned from their work in the class and what rhetoric, composition, and literacy studies scholars can learn from students' conclusions. In both examples, I emphasize students' responses, and (when possible) feature their individual voices in order to begin to address the problem of the absence of students' contributions to academia's and the public's considerations of these issues. My hope is that we (as a field and as academics) can continue to encourage and facilitate student participation in these larger discussions.

The two examples that follow present the work and contributions of my students at the College of Staten Island (CSI). Functioning as both a community college and a senior college in the City University of New York (CUNY) public higher education system, CSI has a unique student body comprised of primarily New York City residents who come from working- or middle-class homes, who are often first-generation college students, and who have a diverse range of racial, ethnic, and cultural backgrounds and educational experiences. Like the nineteenth-century American lyceum, Brookwood Labor College, and the Lindberg Center's basic literacy program, CSI has not been viewed as a site or sponsor of intellectualism. Despite being an institution of higher education, the college's history as a public open-admissions institution and its current hybrid status of community college and senior college contribute to its not being considered a site of intellectualism in the twenty-first century. In fact, a number of students have noted the college often gets referred to as CSI: The College of Stupid Idiots. For these reasons, an examination of CSI students' experiences and views builds on and expands the findings and conclusions of the three case studies highlighted in this book.

"BE STUPID"? THE POPULAR CULTURE ARTIFACT ANALYSIS

The primary writing assignment I have used in my first-year writing courses is what I call a popular culture artifact analysis. The assignment: select a popular culture artifact (for example, a TV show, film, advertisement, commercial, or song) that sends a message about learning, intelligence, intellectualism, or education in American culture; analyze the message it sends; interrogate how it sends that message (the rhetorical strategies used to persuade the audience); and consider how that message may affect society's beliefs and actions. My goal for this assignment is to engage students in exploring their society's views of education and intellectualism as expressed by popular media. I focus on the media because they function as what Henry A. Giroux has called a substantial "educational force" (*The Mouse* 2). Positioning popular culture artifacts as the subject of rhetorical analysis in a composition class can help students critically examine—and consequently challenge—these influential forces mediating views about learning, education, and intellectualism in American culture. This work is particularly relevant for composition classes because popular culture texts are part of the rhetorical situation in which students are being educated and from which they can become participants in the larger discussions of intellectualism and anti-intellectualism.

To prepare students for this analysis, I typically assign a few articles by the scholars and cultural critics cited in chapter 1 who raise some of the primary issues about education and intellectualism that concern young people my students' age. Among the readings I have assigned are Mark Edmundson's "On the Uses of a Liberal Education: As Lite Entertainment for Bored College Students," Nicholas Carr's "Is Google Making Us Stupid?," and Thomas de Zengotita's "The Numbing of the American Mind." I also typically assign an article by Richard Hofstadter ("Democracy and American Anti-Intellectualism") in order to expose students to the historical nature of this rhetoric. I supplement these readings with one or two that model for students the type of popular culture analysis I am asking of them. Those articles include Dianne Williams Hayes's "Athletes, Outcasts, and Partyers," which argues films about African Americans in higher education rarely depict them as anything but athletes, outcasts, or partyers; Aeon Skoble's "Lisa and American Anti-intellectualism," which claims *The Simpsons* sends an anti-intellectual message; and Steven Johnson's "Watching TV Makes You Smarter," in which he contends some television shows require and foster critical thinking.

In addition to discussing the course readings, I prepare students for the written assignment by modeling, with them, the process of rhetorically analyzing a current popular culture artifact. In the past, we have analyzed an episode of the television comedy *Community*, the game show *Are You Smarter Than a Fifth Grader?*, college websites, and a variety of advertisements. Recently, I have used Diesel's "Be Stupid" ad campaign. I discovered the usefulness of this ad campaign for modeling the work of popular culture artifact analysis a few years ago when it produced a surprisingly rich discussion about education, class, and intelligence—a discussion I present now to demonstrate the effectiveness of this assignment in engaging students in a critical analysis of the rhetoric of intellectualism and anti-intellectualism in the United States.[1]

In 2010, the clothing company known as Diesel launched its "Be Stupid" ad campaign—a campaign espousing the philosophy that to "be stupid" means to take risks, to think outside the box, to pursue "a regret-free life." The message—clearly targeted at youth culture—is delivered through ads with playful slogans and provocative images, and a hip video replete with dance-inducing disco rock music. Hinged on the ironic argument that to "be stupid" is actually "smart," Diesel's ad campaign at first seems compelling and refreshing. However, the billboard-style ads, with their life-size text shouting slogans like "Smart May Have the Brains, But Stupid Has the Balls" and their shocking images of bikini-clad young women exposing themselves or young men engaging in dangerous behavior, send more than a "think outside the box" message. These ads equate a regret-free life with "being stupid" and depict that life as one based on destructive, reckless, lewd, and lascivious behavior.

When Diesel released its "Be Stupid" ad campaign, not surprisingly, it received some significant attention immediately. Critics were appalled by the lewd images and the call to "be stupid," while others lauded the company for promoting uniqueness, thinking outside the box, and fun. I encountered the ads a few years ago as I was walking through the subway tunnels in Manhattan. On my long walk to the subway exit, I was greeted by the "Be Stupid" mantra again and again, along with a plethora of sibling slogans like "Trust Stupid," "I'm with Stupid," "Stupid Is Spreading," "Think Less. More Stupid," and "Smart had one good idea and that idea was stupid." I was repeatedly startled not only by the slogans but also by the accompanying images of young women exposing themselves and poised in provocative positions and young men walking confidently away from destruction, engaging in dangerous behavior with a smile, and behaving lasciviously.

A few days after running into these ads, I brought them into the composition class I was teaching at the time because we were just beginning the popular culture artifact analysis unit. That particular semester the theme of the course was American popular culture at large (not the rhetoric of intellectualism and anti-intellectualism), so the assignment was broader: to analyze a popular culture artifact for the messages (any) it was sending to its audience. After encountering the Diesel ads, however, I thought they would be a good example of a current popular media artifact we could use to practice as a class the type of analysis the writing assignment was asking of students. Because the rhetoric of anti-intellectualism and intellectualism was not the theme of the course, this particular class of students had not read Hofstadter or any of the other articles I typically assign. We had also not discussed the topic prior to my bringing in the Diesel ads for group discussion.

Entering the classroom that day, I assumed students would find the ads funny and effective and that I would have to nudge them a bit to analyze the rhetoric of the campaign (something I've experienced often when facilitating an analytical discussion like this). To my surprise, an often-quiet class could not say enough about the ads—and none of it was positive. They were surprised and angered by the ads—ads they confessed they had never seen. After showing them several of the ads, I played for them the video available on the Diesel website titled "The Official Be Stupid Philosophy." After watching the video twice, students pointed out it was absent any of the images found in the ads and that the overall message seemed motivational with statements including the following: "Like balloons we are filled with hopes and dreams but over time a single sentence creeps into our lives: Don't be stupid. It's the crusher of possibility. It's the world's greatest deflator," "Stupid is the relentless pursuit of a regret-free life," "Stupid isn't afraid to fail," and "The fact is if we didn't have stupid thoughts we'd have no interesting thoughts at all."

After discussing the video, we returned to the ads. I urged students to explain, in rhetorical terms, what they disliked about the ads. After all, the pathetic appeal of sexually explicit ads is nothing new. When we talked about the message of the video and the text in the ads, the students acknowledged that the ironic tone of the slogans could be interpreted as a positive logical argument for being creative and bucking conformity, but they felt the visual representation of this "think outside the box" message rested on a completely different pathetic appeal. To them, the images, alongside the text, seemed to be arguing that for women to be "stupid" (or, in other words, smart, creative, cool), they need to take their clothes off, position themselves provocatively, and emphasize their bodies over their brains. For men to be equally "stupid," they must be destructive, reckless, aggressive, funny, and engage with women's bodies, not their brains.

I was still a bit surprised that my students were making these arguments and were not telling me or each other that they were "reading too much" into the ads. I nudged them further to see why they didn't identify with these ads at all. Their age group was, in fact, the target audience. When we looked at who, according to the ads, was "smart enough to be stupid" (one of the campaign slogans is, in fact, "Are you smart enough to be stupid?"), the students noticed that all the models (except two) were white. They also informed me that they don't buy Diesel jeans because they are really expensive. Products of working- and middle-class families of mixed races and ethnicities and enrolled in an open-admissions public college, my students were saying they couldn't "see" themselves in the ads and they knew they couldn't afford the clothes. For them, the ads indicated that the people who can afford to "be stupid" are white middle- to upper-class youth with the privilege of a good education and exceptional financial support that would not prevent them from gaining access to the resources and cultural capital they desired. My students did not possess such security. When I told them where I saw the ads (the West 4th Street subway stop in Manhattan), they quickly noted that was the subway station near New York University. Perhaps, they said, NYU students could identify with the ads.

This in-class exercise engaged students in thoughtful, critical exploration of the consumer-driven culture "educating" them on issues related to intellectualism, intelligence, youth, and class. What I noticed in the artifact analysis essays the students composed following this discussion was their willingness and ability to recognize the social, cultural, and economic messages that popular media send. They also were more apt to see how popular media can influence their own and others' views of intelligence, intellectualism, and education. I have continued to use Diesel's ad campaign in class to model the popular culture artifact analysis with my students at CSI, and it has produced similar conversations. (It would be fruitful, I think, to see what kind of analysis it would produce at schools with students who are more readily represented in the ad campaign.) Because of the success of this particular assignment and because I recognized the importance of getting students to examine the rhetoric of anti-intellectualism and intellectualism in the United States beyond popular culture media's contributions, I recently designed a first-year writing course that explored the issue more broadly and for an entire semester. That course is the focus of my second example of teaching the rhetoric of intellectualism and anti-intellectualism to first-year writing students.

THE DUMBEST GENERATION? A SEMESTER-LONG STUDY

> Lucinda[2]: I felt as though [the author] was right in comparing the college environment to that of a consumer culture, where we, the students, are more focused on getting our money's worth, than

> on the exploration of new studies and ideas. . . . We, as a society, are just too focused on consumer goods, and college is turning into just that.
>
> Kawsar: We all feel that getting good grades is a must if we want to graduate, continue our education and even pursue the career we have always dreamed of as kids; thus, the idea of trying out new courses and later realizing that the courses did not work out too well, scares us and is perhaps the biggest reason many of us tend to shy away from taking classes we think may be interesting.
>
> Gina: In our current economical state, I believed it prudent to put finances before my education in college. In this day and time even college isn't enough. In order to secure a job in most fields of study, graduate school is almost a necessity. We are now groomed from a young age to do everything we can to become successful. College has become just another part of the plan. It is no longer about knowledge and obtaining "critical thinking" skills. It is about money and success. . . . I do not feel as if college is about obtaining an education. . . . I do believe that the commercialism of college is the driving force.
>
> Joseph: I agree with what Gina has to say about it being "prudent to put finances before my education in college." In the current economic state that we live in today choosing a college to attend has become even more difficult. During my own experience with picking a college I found that I wasn't going to be able to attend my top choice private school because it was too expensive. The price of college became the basis for what I picked a school on.

The student discussion board comments above are representative of the sentiments expressed by my students in an honors first-year composition course I recently taught that focused on examining and responding to widespread public rhetoric accusing Americans (especially young ones) of being anti-intellectual and ignorant. Interestingly, students' work over the semester revealed that despite being part of a prestigious honors program that softens the economic hardship of college and provides a unique set of academic opportunities, they view higher education in consumerist—rather than academic—terms. While this sentiment may not be surprising at large, especially given the economic climate in which today's students are pouring their (or their parents') money into a college education,[3] it is particularly telling when it comes from students receiving benefits like waived tuition costs, a free laptop, early registration opportunities, access to advanced seminars solely for honors students, low course caps, and mentoring and study-abroad opportunities. In fact, the honors program these students are a part of claims it

> provides outstanding educational opportunities, advising and financial support, the tools our most talented students need to excel in this area and the world, in college and in life. Selected for their top high school records and leadership potential, each . . . student is awarded a full-tuition merit scholarship, giving them the freedom to pursue their academic goals without financial burdens. (*Macaulay Honors College*)

In what follows, I introduce and summarize the course assignments and activities and highlight what students say they learned from the coursework. I cite heavily students in their own words in an effort to bring their voices to the forefront of our field's considerations of the rhetoric of intellectualism and anti-intellectualism in the United States. As I noted earlier, my hope is that we can extend student participation in these discussions within and beyond our own field.

The Course

Honors composition at CSI is a one-semester composition course exclusively for students in the Macaulay Honors Program (approximately forty students are accepted into the program a year and they are divided into two sections of composition). The purpose of the course is to help students develop their college-level critical reading, writing, and research skills. Professors teaching the course have the freedom to design the course as they wish, as long as they meet the course objectives, which are the same for the non-honors sections. It is implied, however, that the professor will assign more challenging readings and writing assignments, commensurate with an honors-level course.

While I have typically contained the focus on the rhetoric of anti-intellectualism to one unit (out of three or four) for a course, in this case I chose to make it the focus of the entire semester's work, titling the course "The Dumbest Generation? Analyzing the Rhetoric of American Anti-intellectualism and Ignorance." I divided the semester into four units, each with a different thematic focus and a different set of rhetorical, writing, and research skills as the objective. I selected the units, readings, and writing assignments I did because they represented some of the primary facets of contemporary accusations of anti-intellectualism and ignorance most relevant to my students: what it means to be intellectual or anti-intellectual, the state of education in the United States, the influence of popular media, technology's influence on learning and literacy, anti-intellectualism in politics, and the role of class and race in learning and intellectualism. In addition, the readings varied in length, difficulty, methodology, and argument, and the writing assignments got progressively longer and built on the reading, writing, and research skills required in the previous paper. I asked students to see their classmates and me as the primary audience for their coursework. In what follows, I describe briefly each unit, along with the readings and major writing assignment associated with it.

Unit 1: Beliefs about Education and Intellectualism. For this, the first major paper, I asked students to use their reading and our discussion of Thomas de Zengotita's "The Numbing of the American Mind," Mark Edmundson's "On the Uses of a Liberal Education: As Lite Entertainment for Bored College Students," Richard Hofstadter's "Democracy and Anti-intellectualism," and an NPR interview with Richard Arum (one of the authors of *Academically Adrift*) to help them think about their own views of education or intellectualism. The issues raised in the readings included what it means to be an intellectual or to be anti-intellectual, what students' attitudes toward college education are, how universities and professors contribute to or impede the learning that takes place at college, the extent to which the American public engages with ideas (or remains numb to them), and the social and cultural factors that affect Americans' attitudes toward learning and education.

For the paper I asked students to select one of these issues to reflect critically on, drawing on their personal experiences, insights, opinions, beliefs, and ideas to support their claims. I wanted to begin the semester with students reflecting on their own views so they were more aware of them as they encountered later readings that discussed critics' assessments of the causes and consequences of anti-intellectual sentiments. Several students wrote about their own definitions of intellectualism while others wrote about their learning experiences in high school and college. Students' consumerist and career-driven attitudes about education surfaced immediately in this first paper.

Unit 2: The Role of Popular Media. For the second unit, I wanted students to examine one of the most pervasive public influences on young Americans' views of education and intellectualism: popular media. This is the popular culture artifact analysis assignment discussed earlier in the chapter. The texts we read and discussed as a class for this unit included Dianne Williams Hayes's "Athletes, Outcasts, and Partyers," Aeon Skoble's "Lisa and Anti-intellectualism," Dane Claussen's "A Brief History of Anti-intellectualism in American Media," and Steven Johnson's "Watching TV Makes You Smarter."

Unit 3: Politics and Technology. At the heart of the third unit was an examination of two issues that surface in many of the contemporary critiques of the American mind: the relationship between technology and intellectualism (in and out of the classroom), and the relationship between politics and anti-intellectualism. The articles we read and discussed for this unit included Nicholas Carr's "Is Google Making Us Stupid?," Jamais Cascio's "Get Smarter," Todd Gitlin's "The Renaissance of Anti-intellectualism," and Elvin T. Lim's "Five Trends in Presidential Rhetoric." We also watched portions of the Frontline video *Digital Nation: Life on the Virtual Frontier.*

The paper I assigned for this unit asked students to "weigh in" on (or enter) a conversation about one of these two issues. For this essay they had to summarize (briefly) at least two sources speaking to the issue they chose and "weigh in" with their own opinion, supporting it by analyzing the texts and by drawing upon their experiences or other outside knowledge. Students had the option to either research the topic on their own and select two nonassigned readings for the paper or they could select one course reading and find a second noncourse reading. A majority of students wrote about the relationship between technology and intellectualism; a few took up the issue of politics and anti-intellectualism.

Unit 4: Analytical Research. This final paper, the analytical research paper, asked students to investigate in more depth some aspect of the course theme (their choice) they wanted to understand more fully. I asked them to conduct both traditional secondary scholarly research on their topic and also, on a small scale, conduct some form of qualitative primary research (including surveys, questionnaires, interviews, etc.). There was no particular subtheme for this unit, but we did discuss a few additional readings that helped us consider the role of race and class in issues of education and intellectualism. We read Earl Shorris's "On the Uses of a Liberal Education: As a Weapon in the Hands of the Restless Poor" and listened to an online radio interview with Mike Rose, discussing his book *The Mind at Work: Valuing the Intelligence of the American Worker.* Shorris proposes that what the poor need is exposure to the humanities, and he shares stories of some students for whom taking free courses in the humanities led to greater self-esteem, to more effective conflict resolution, and for many, to going to college. Rose argues we need to recognize the cognitive skills required of many blue-collar jobs and value the intelligence of these workers. Both texts, I thought, would challenge the students to look beyond their primarily middle-class experiences to consider the value of education and intellectualism for the working-class and working poor.

A number of students chose to explore further either technology's or popular media's influence on their generation; others researched the causes of changes in presidential rhetoric, whether colleges are really enriching young people's minds, and whether the education system in another country has had different results from the American system.

The Study and Methodology

As I was designing this course, I applied for and received IRB approval with my institution to ask students for their consent to analyze and cite in future publications their primary coursework (papers and online reflection posts on the assigned readings). I also asked for permission to invite interested students to complete a post-course survey reflecting on the design and theme of the course and to ask for their consent to cite their responses. Though I had originally planned to contact students immediately after course grades had been posted at the end of the semester, I decided to wait some time before asking the students if they would be interested in participating.

I contacted the entire class eight months after the course had ended and student grades were posted, inviting them to participate in my research. Five of the twenty students responded and agreed to complete a short survey and let me quote their course materials and their surveys. I decided to wait eight months to contact students because I was interested in how much students retained from the course and because I wanted their comments to be distanced from their initial investment (especially in terms of a grade) in the course. I discuss now my findings and share excerpts from students' reflections and contributions.

The Findings

Based on student coursework and the reflections five students provided eight months after the completion of the honors composition course, students felt the coursework helped them (1) become aware of what has influenced their views about learning and education, including popular media, their high school experiences, and economic realities; (2) develop their views, beliefs, and attitudes toward education and intellectualism; and (3) express how their experiences challenge some of the accusations of anti-intellectualism and ignorance.

Understanding Influence. For the popular media artifact analysis (Essay 2), students selected a variety of TV shows, films, and advertisements to analyze. While most students argued that the artifact they selected sends a negative message about education or intellectualism and perpetuates stereotypes about intellectualism and anti-intellectualism, some recognized that their artifacts send positive or mixed messages. A few students noticed their artifacts sent different messages about the expectations and consequences of intellectualism depending on gender, race, or age. Several students, both in their essays and in their post-course surveys, recognized the influence such popular media had on their and their classmates' perceptions of intellectualism and anti-intellectualism. Discussing what she learned from writing the popular media analysis paper, Lucinda wrote on her survey,

> From Essay #2, I learned that the debate of intellectualism versus anti-intellectualism is very prevalent in the media, and the media shapes these different definitions to fit their stereotypes. Intellectuals are typically awkward, nerdy, very smart and have few friends whereas the anti-intellectuals are beautiful, popular, have many friends, and are of average or little intelligence. These stereotypes extend to all networks and all age ranges. . . . My essay focused on *The Big Bang Theory*, and by taking a close look at the show, it was not hard to see that the media heavily addresses these stereotypes in the show and will continue to do so in the future.

Similarly, Dhiwya wrote in her survey that she realized how much her own definitions of *intellectual* and *anti-intellectual* were influenced by the media. She saw this among her peers, too, when she did her primary research for the analytical research paper at the end of the semester:

> For my analytical research paper I studied whether or not the portrayal of intellects and anti-intellects in mass media and pop culture had any affect [*sic*] on the perception of these groups of people by the average person by surveying a small group of college students. In television, movies, radio shows, tabloids, and other forms of entertainment seen by millions upon millions of people, many of them share a common trait when it comes to their portrayal of the intellect and anti-intellect especially in an educational setting. When I conducted my survey I had the

> students draw their idea of an intellect/anti-intellect, describe in words their definition of each, and give some examples of people associated with each group that were part of pop culture. When it came to the drawings, the depictions went almost hand in hand to the stereotypical views of these groups of people as depicted by the media. The intellects were usually shown as the nerdy geek type (with the exception of the intellect being a female in which case they were seen as slightly more attractive than their male counterparts) and the anti-intellects were fat, and ugly when it came to the males, and rich, and snotty when it came to the females. All this matched up with traits of intellects and anti-intellects seen in the media especially the people and characters named for each group. However, when it came to the definition of each group of people, the definitions told a different story. In most cases, the intellects were described as smart, innovative, and generally desirable people to be while the anti-intellect was not so desirably described. This showed me that although we may think one way (that being an intellect is not demeaning and being an anti-intellect is not very desirable) when it came to the physical depiction of them, it went more in line with what the media showed.

Dhiwya's findings are particularly interesting because she examined her peers' visual perceptions in conjunction with their definitions, which revealed a significant inconsistency. In other words, while what it means to be an intellectual may be appealing to students, how intellectuals are portrayed in the media make being one less desirable. Notably, the activity Dhiwya used for her primary research (having her peers draw their perceptions of intellectualism and anti-intellectualism) was one I used with her class early on in the semester, prior to the unit focused on popular media. Students' in-class drawings showed the same trends Dhiwya and Lucinda recognized in their research. The class sample revealed the following breakdown of stereotypes: anti-intellectual young women are anti-intellectual because they are obsessed with vanity and consumerism; male anti-intellectuals are couch potatoes. Intellectual men tended to look like professors and intellectual young women were glasses-wearing book readers. When students wrote their artifact analyses a few weeks after we did this activity in class, these same stereotypes were present in their artifacts, indicating students' contact with media stereotypes influence their assumptions.

Dhiwya's in-class depiction of anti-intellectualism

Student interest in the influence of popular media on public perceptions of intellectualism and anti-intellectualism and its role in fostering attitudes and beliefs about learning was evident when eight out of twenty students (40 percent) made it the subject of their final research paper. Among the questions they explored in their research were, "Does TV make us smarter or impair our cognitive skills?"; "Just how much of our ideas of how an intellect would look and behave is molded by what we see in pop culture?"; "What effects are the portrayals of teen girls in films targeted at teens having on gender stereotypes and intellectualism?"; and "Are there trends in TV punditry that can lead to anti-intellectualism?" While they all concluded that the media had significant influence, even more interesting is that students were interested in investigating these questions, especially in relation to their personal experiences and interests.

Developing Views. Students' survey comments also demonstrated that they thought the coursework helped them develop or alter their own views or thinking about intellectualism and education. Joseph wrote in the survey,

Joseph's in-class depiction of intellectualism

Before taking this class I had not thought about or studied intellectualism or anti-intellectualism in any way. I had seen and heard from media outlets, such as the nightly news, that people had been claiming that my age group was the "dumbest generation," but I had never pursued any research on the subject. My beliefs about intellectualism and anti-intellectualism prior to this class were very basic. I had the thought in my head that there were only people who were considered smart, successful, and leaders (the intellectuals) and people who couldn't think for him or herself and were in a way considered to be a bit vapid (the anti-intellectuals). As you can see, my beliefs weren't the most complex; however, by the end of the semester I had learned that there are so many opinions and vantage points that people take when it comes to his or her own beliefs on intellectualism and anti-intellectualism. These two terms aren't exactly black and white, but rather it comes down to, according to Richard Hofstadter, whether a person is living for ideas or living off of ideas, to determine if they are an intellectual or anti-intellectual. . . . After taking this class my views

> on intellectualism more developed than changed. By developed, I mean to say that they grew and expanded as a result of the little information I had on the topic to begin with. Our class gave everyone an extremely in-depth look into the ideas surrounding intellectualism, and this is what ultimately changed my views from being a very basic understanding to being well rounded on the arguments surrounding the term "intellectualism."

As he states, Joseph learned that his peers and even the scholars we read define intellectualism and anti-intellectualism differently. By the end of the semester, he seemed to most agree with Hofstadter's definitions and tended to use his definitions as his lens for considering the images and critiques he encountered. Other students maintained their own personal definitions or simply acknowledged that there is no one true definition for these terms but that the definitions reflect the intentions and expectations of the definers. This, I believe, is an important lesson for students. Also significant in Joseph's response is that he doesn't claim the course, or the coursework, *changed* his views—something I worried students might assume they needed to claim when responding to the survey. His recognition that his beliefs didn't change, but became more informed, is a testament to his confidence and ownership of his own beliefs.

One of the primary issues about which students appeared to develop their beliefs was the role of technology in promoting or inhibiting intellectualism—inside and outside the classroom. In fact, thirteen of the twenty students (65 percent) chose this topic for their third essay (over politics) and six out of twenty (30 percent) made this the focus of their research paper, asking questions like "Is Facebook detrimental to academic success?"; "Has technology made us less intellectual?"; "Does technology help or hinder education?"; and "Are video games having a positive or negative effect on intellectualism?"

Following the course readings and the Frontline video *Digital Nation*, students understood the contentious nature of the debate about the influence of technology on young minds—some critics firmly on the "technology is bad" side and others planted solidly in the "technology is good" camp. In our discussions, students expressed genuine concern about how technology was affecting their generation, particularly how it might be affecting them personally. This issue, in fact, appeared to be an aspect of the larger debate between intellectualism and anti-intellectualism that they most connected with and saw as most relevant to their lives. To compare, while they recognized and researched the influence of popular media representations, they didn't appear as *concerned* by it as they were by the influence of technologies like the Internet, computers, smartphones, video games, etc.

Lucinda expressed her interest in the topic this way:

> For this class, I was more interested in the digital aspect of the course; in other words, how society is changing due to the technology that continually surrounds us and plans our every move. The readings that led me down that road were "The Numbing of the American Mind" and the online video *Digital Nation: Life on the Virtual Frontier.* These struck me more than the others because I am very fascinated in psychology and how new inventions can affect the minds of individuals that use them, and eventually society as a whole. Because I am a part of the generation who grew up with the Internet, I want to know what it is doing to me and other people my age in terms of side effects and psychological dependences.

Interesting in Lucinda's comment is the assumption (and concern that) technology is "doing" something to her and her peers. Andrew Feenberg, in *Critical Theory of Technology*, described this problematic view as the "substantive" view of technology: seeing technology as "an autonomous cultural force" (5) with the power to control and damage us. This view is in contrast to the equally problematic "instrumentalist view" of technology that unquestioningly embraces it. Feenberg, instead, argued for the "critical theory" view of technology that recognizes technology as a process people can and should be involved in.

Evident in their essays, students were working through the "substantive" and "instrumentalist" views they were encountering in their research on the topic. Consequently, their essays tended to be structured as pro-and-con analyses. While the student who researched the effects of Facebook concluded that the effects were primarily negative, all other students felt the influence of the technology they were exploring was more positive than negative. Tellingly, though, they also claimed that the issue is complex, the effects aren't fully knowable yet, and individuals and teachers must take responsibility for how they engage with these technologies. For example, after considering her interviews with several students and professors and her library research, Lucinda concluded her essay by saying,

> From the evidence, I believe that technology can be helpful in the college classroom, but only when used correctly. Professors need to understand the technology they are using first and figure out

> what is best to use for the subject that they are teaching. If they can find a balance, then students will benefit greatly from their class.

Kawsar, who investigated the same topic (technology in the classroom), had a similar conclusion:

> As of now . . . it seems that technology has held a more beneficial role in education. . . . However, our education systems must not "forget" that it is our teachers and administrators who manipulate the extent to how and which technology they incorporate—not technology "directing" our staff to use it if it is useless. And who knows? If people abuse what was intentionally meant to serve as an educational supplement, the opposite result may occur in the near future.

What Lucinda's and Kawsar's (and their peers') comments indicated was that by the end of the semester they understood better and had become more critically aware of the public's and their own competing views of technology. While students did not exhaust the debate and had not reached the "critical theory" view of technology Feenberg promotes, they were developing their views by building their knowledge base about the issue.

Speaking Back. The most prominent trend in students' coursework and reflections was that while they agreed with some of the criticisms of their generation, they were able and willing to critique assumptions that their generation is necessarily ignorant and anti-intellectual. Their thoughtful critiques demonstrate that through a semester of studying discourses of intellectualism and anti-intellectualism, examining influential forces, and developing their own views, students became more prepared to speak back to and challenge those discourses.

Many in the class understood why some of the authors described students as "academically adrift," "the dumbest generation," or academically "lazy," but they believe strongly that the reason for this state of affairs is the larger social, cultural, and economic context that surrounds them. They respond to the criticisms, consequently, with experiential explanations for why these negative perceptions are incomplete. Dhiwya articulated this in her explanation of what she learned from writing the first paper,

> [The education analysis] paper allowed me to really understand why there is such a drastic sense of "anti-intellectualism" in American education. When it comes to why people go to college in the modern age, it is almost always in order to pursue a career that will

> give them the kind of salary that will allow for a comfortable life. People are not going to college necessarily for the sole purpose of gaining knowledge and expanding their horizons even though this may have been the original reason for colleges when they first came to be, to allow for the growth of intellect in society's rich and elite with all the time to spare. Now, however, time is a luxury that most people just do not have. They must spend it wisely to learn what they must and usually not much more. This fact does not make America less intellectual it just means the society that we live in doesn't make the pursuit of intellect an easy thing to do and just because some students are unable to spare some of their precious time to gain intellect, it does not make them anti-intellectuals.

Dhiwya's comment sounds similar to Kawsar's statement quoted at the beginning of this section—that students are necessarily so focused on the courses they need to take and getting good grades that the idea of college as a place for intellectual exploration seems unrealistic to them.

Many of these types of comments originated when students, early in the semester, read Mark Edmundson's 1997 *Harper's* article "On the Uses of a Liberal Education: As Lite Entertainment for Bored College Students." Despite the article being fifteen years old, students agreed with Edmundson's argument that college has become an economic stepping stone in a consumer-driven world. In his words, "It's that university culture, like American culture writ large, is, to put it crudely, ever more devoted to consumption and entertainment, to the using and using up of goods and images" (40). Among the consequences he cites are passionless, uncritical students; colleges marketing themselves to students and parents on their nonacademic attributes rather than their academic ones, and universities failing in their intellectual mission (42–43).

Many students agreed with Edmundson, acknowledging that, in their experience so far, higher education lacks an emphasis on intellectualism and critical thinking, and students' motivation is not an intellectual one. For Dhiwya, those sentiments begin with the message that students receive about education before even going to college. In her online reading response to Edmundson's piece, she wrote,

> I agree with [my classmate] when she says that universities "are not the lone factor to the sad intellectual state of American students." Instead we have to look back to high school, or even further back

> to when standardized tests, SATS's [*sic*] and resumes were the pieces of information that defined us. So, from a young age we were taught that these things were what mattered the most; these things were what was going to separate me from the other millions of students. We "commit so much time and effort, slaving away for one goal" that when we enter college, it might be hard to break from the traditional, "study what's in the textbook, learn the facts and move on." All through high school I would hear that once I entered college, I would be nothing but a number to the professors so what would matter would be my test scores. So when we enter small classrooms that encourage deeper analytical thinking, it might not be so easy to get these ideas out.

Dhiwya's assessment accords with critiques of education like Diane Ravitch's assessment of the No Child Left Behind (NCLB) curriculum, a curriculum Dhiwya and her classmates would have been schooled under. According to Ravitch, because of the emphasis on basic skills and improved test scores, the NCLB curriculum

> produced mountains of data, not educated citizens. Its advocates then treated that data as evidence of its "success." It ignored the importance of knowledge. It promoted a cramped, mechanistic, profoundly anti-intellectual definition of education. In the age of NCLB, knowledge was irrelevant. (29)

In short, she claims, our contemporary teaching methods are creating a student body who associate school with testing, not learning (231).

Gina, in her education analysis essay, tied students' actions in college to the larger economic state and to our culture's definition of success. She wrote,

> In this day and age, success and wealth are extremely important to maintaining a stable life. One cannot savor their time in college. In this fast paced world, we rarely have the luxury of fostering intellectual pursuits. And if we do, it is usually more of a bonus and not the main goal. College is only one stop we make on our path to success. And those four years (or possibly more) . . . are barely significant in the grand scheme of things. As sad as it is, we must conform to fit the times in order to achieve the success we desire. . . . From childhood, we are taught that attaining success and wealth are essential components for happiness. We are given tools for success and, in my case, characterized as "intelligent"

> from a young age. Even as children, we are led to believe that money and success are interchangeable. And that idea, maybe not consciously, sticks with us through adulthood. These goals and generalizations render us unable to recognize the real purpose of obtaining an education: learning. Although one cannot argue that school teaches us valuable lessons, these lessons may not be the ones we should be learning. And as we advance these lessons become more and more convoluted. School becomes less and less about "learning." We become more and more focused on the idea of success. And in today's day and age, there is only one path. College.

Gina's comments also resonate with many critiques of contemporary education, including Mike Rose's description in *Why School? Reclaiming Education for All of Us*. In his words,

> For some time now, our national discussion of education has been dominated by a language of test scores and economic competitiveness. To be sure, a major goal of American education is to prepare the young to make a living. But parents send their kids to school for many other reasons as well: intellectual, social, civic, ethical, aesthetic. Historically, these justifications for schooling have held more importance. Not today. (4)

Likewise, in their critique of higher education, the authors of *Academically Adrift* blame a "market-based logic of education" for students' "instrumental" views of education (16). The authors cite historical sociologist David Labree's claim that "we have credentialism to thank for aversions to learning that, to a great extent, lies at the heart of our educational system" (qtd. in Arum and Roska 16). These views, as evident in my students' comments, are affecting the way young people think about education and the choices they make in their pursuit of education.

Unlike some of his peers, Joseph agreed with some accusations that college students today *are* anti-intellectual:

> The need of a college degree has created an influx of students that often are not there to gain a higher education or enhance their own knowledge, but solely based on the fact that they believe they need to be there in order to get a job. These people are the anti-intellectuals, according to Hofstadter; they are attending college because it is the idea that society has influenced upon them. Hofstadter

> defines an anti-intellectual as someone who lives off of ideas, as well as being suspicious and having a sort of resentment towards intellectuals (282). This does not mean that the anti-intellectual is not intelligent; it is stating that these people solely live off the standards set up by society. Meaning, that they never challenge the normalities of society or question what they are doing; they act in a way they believe is the acceptable way to act and think. The anti-intellectual does things because he or she believe it to be the correct thing to do and it is what society wants, as compared to the intellectual who lives to think critically and challenge the standards set by society around them. College has become a place where the anti-intellectual thrives, where it is all about receiving the college degree everyone needs for a job, and not about intellectual growth.

Joseph's use of Richard Hofstadter's definition of anti-intellectualism reflects his thoughtful critique of today's college students. Not calling them "dumb" (as some critics do), he demonstrates how the current prevailing notion that all young people must go to college solely to get a job fosters anti-intellectual views of higher education.

Kawsar also agreed with some of the critiques and offers this explanation:

> But, the truth of the matter is that many students are getting lazier. Perhaps even less intellectual. But not dumb. In fact, it seems that more and more students are becoming anti-intellectual because thinking comes to them as a burden, and not as a way to exercise the mind. In fact, Richard Hofstadter captures this idea when he says, ". . . Ours is a society in which every form of play seems to be accepted by the majority except the play of the mind" (Hofstadter 285). Being that his article, "Democracy and Anti-Intellectualism in America" was written over half a century ago, to us the reason Hofstadter says this may be unclear. But if we apply his statement to today's world, we can blame the dwindling intellectualism of students on technological advancements, which, in so many ways, make our lives simpler and more convenient. Because these modern marvels make post secondary education more resourceful and more accessible, higher education is more readily available for a larger range of students, which, in effect, makes competition fiercer than ever before. Many students just want to memorize material, spit it back on the test paper, get a good grade, move on to whatever comes next, and forget previous material in order to

> be better qualified for candidacy in higher-education institutions. But, the question that comes up here is why? Why do students feel the need get flawless grades despite having not learned anything? Based on several class discussions, the answer to that question comes down to four words: To get a job.

Like Joseph, Kawsar says today's students are not dumb, but they are driven by the equation of college with getting a job and by competing with their peers because of increased access to higher education.

Challenging those critics who blame technology for creating "the dumbest generation" (including Carr and Bauerlein), Dhiwya offered an explanation. Her explanation is implied in her description of what she learned from writing the critical "weigh-in" essay:

> This paper allowed me to realize the effects of technology on intellect and anti-intellect. While some argued that the constant availability of information and the declining need to memorize has led to a decrease in intellect I believe that it has just changed the way we think and apply our knowledge to adapt to the changing environment. Because of modern technology, practically any piece of information we require is available to us with a quick look in any search engine. However, with the addition of this technology "intellects" do not really memorize but rather utilize the resources at their disposal and develop something innovative with it. In this way I believe that technology has not had a deleterious effect on the intellect of people as a whole, but rather a beneficial one. People may not have the same set of skills they did a decade ago that was associated with an intellect, but the new skills that have replaced the old have also allowed men to create many new and better things for society, in a way becoming a sort of modern intellect.

In this reflection, Dhiwya makes an important point that perhaps we need to reconsider what it means to be intellectual in the twenty-first century, taking into consideration changes in modern learning and thinking practices. And perhaps she is right.

The students quoted here (and their classmates), of course, represent a particular category of college student: the honor student. Noted earlier, they are students who applied for and were accepted into an honors program that grants them financial and academic advantages other students don't receive. Also, selected for their academic success prior to college and for their demonstration of leadership potential, they represent a small portion of today's college students. As many of them noted in their comments throughout the semester, like many honors students, they felt pressure in high school from families and schools to push themselves, to always get good grades, and to build up an impressive resume; the honors program also requires that they maintain a particularly high GPA. The pressure for good grades and academic success they have experienced has certainly contributed to their attitudes toward education and their intellectual experiences.

These students also represent a unique set of honors students. For instance, despite the prestigious reputation of the honors program itself, these students are attending a college that is not considered intellectual or elite. Consequently, my students' experiences and responses may be influenced by the contradictory reputations of the college they are attending and the honors program they participate in. These students are also unique in that they typically live at home with their parents because housing in New York City is particularly pricey. They also come from primarily middle-class families for whom the cost of college is a burden. As Joseph noted in his statement at the beginning of this piece, he actually decided to attend CSI and be part of the honors program for financial reasons. CSI was not, he stated, his first choice.

Reading students' contributions in the context of this particular student body's experiences prompts us to ask whether non-honors students might offer similar contributions if they participated in a similar course. How might their responses differ? How might honors students at institutions demographically different from those at CSI respond? What challenges to intellectualism do different types of students from different types of institutions face? How do the cultural, economic, and educational pressures other students face cultivate anti-intellectual sentiments or encourage intellectual ones? In the case of these particular students, it seems clear that society is not encouraging or rewarding the pursuit of intellectualism—not even for students participating in a prestigious honors program.

It is also true that because the students in both this course-long study of the rhetoric of intellectualism and anti-intellectualism in the United States and those who participated in the popular culture artifact analysis discussed earlier are first-year freshman, their ideas and attitudes about education and college reflect limited participation in the college experience. It's possible their ideas and attitudes might change as they move into more of their major classes and as they are able to more fully experience the academic opportunities the college affords them. Perhaps further research on students' attitudes and experiences later in their college careers can shed additional light on this issue.

STUDENTS AS CRITICAL CONSUMERS AND CONTRIBUTORS

This chapter has presented two experiments in engaging first-year writing students in the analysis of the rhetoric of intellectualism and anti-intellectualism in the United States. Reflecting on both examples, what strikes me most are students' honest consideration of their past and present experiences; their awareness of the real connection for them among economic security, jobs, and education; and their balanced approach to the critiques of their generation. In their discussion of Diesel's "Be Stupid" ad campaign, students could recognize the appeal of the "be stupid" philosophy, but were also critical enough to recognize that they weren't in the position to "be stupid" and still have success. Willing to recognize many of today's college students have primarily (or solely) consumerist, nonintellectual motivations for attending college, students in the semester-long course offer a thoughtful list of contemporary educational, technological, and economic causes for such attitudes.

It is this type of critical reflection and analysis that rhetoric and composition scholars have long called for literacy educators to foster. Ira Shor, for instance, has argued for a critical pedagogy that helps students develop a "critical curiosity about society, power, inequality, and change" and empowers them to recognize (and challenge) the problematic ways in which their own experiences connect to and are affected by larger social issues and the "social and cultural context of education" (*Empowering* 15, 31). In accord, James Berlin argued for teaching students to critique and resist the discourses working to influence them (52) and called teachers to give students the tools to critique the socially constructed, politically charged reality of classroom, college, and culture (93).

Surely the widespread rhetoric accusing Americans (particularly young Americans) of anti-intellectualism and ignorance is among the most significant and powerful rhetoric influencing our students today. As these two experiments demonstrate, students can benefit from studying this rhetoric because it can deepen their understanding of the causes and consequences of the critiques of their generation, and because it can empower them to respond to the rhetoric—to think critically about their own and their peers' attitudes and actions regarding literacy and learning. As a field, I contend, we should find ways (my popular culture artifact analysis assignment and full course design are only two examples) to engage students with this rhetoric and to equip them to navigate their education empowered by the knowledge that this rhetoric does not have to define them, their views, or their choices.

At a time when narrow notions of intellectualism and a rhetoric of anti-intellectualism loom large, we need to respond as Mike Rose has proposed:

> We need public talk that links education to a more decent, thoughtful, open society. Talk that raises in us as a people the appreciation for deliberation and reflection, or for taking intellectual risks and thinking widely—for the sheer power and pleasure of using our minds, alone or in concert with others. We need a discourse that inspires young people to think gracefully and moves young adults to become teachers and foster such development. (*Why School?* 28–29)

Reimagining Popular Notions of American Intellectualism is an important first step in changing "public talk" about education. Arguing for a definition of intellectualism that values interest in, appreciation for, and engagement with learning, knowledge, deliberation, critical thinking, and inquiry, it works to democratize the term and expand the learning spaces and activities valued by Americans. Through its reexamination of the nineteenth-century lyceum, a twentieth-century labor college, and a twenty-first-century basic literacy program, it demonstrates that despite widespread beliefs that a majority of Americans are anti-intellectual, Americans have engaged and continue to engage in intellectual inquiry and practice. And finally, as this chapter has shown, rhetoric, composition, and literacy studies scholars can help change the rhetoric by encouraging and empowering students to contribute to academic and public conversations that shape how Americans define intellectualism and how they understand the relationship between literacy and twenty-first-century intellectualism. Students' contributions to the debates about intellectualism in American culture help paint a larger picture of the educational, economic, and cultural factors affecting education and intellectualism in the United States today, and they should become part of academic and public discourse concerning these issues.

Notes

Bibliography

Index

Notes

Introduction

1. Wendell is a pseudonym. I have altered the names of the GED students discussed here and later in the book to respect the confidentiality of their identities and their stories.
2. In his history of nonformal adult education in the United States, Joseph Kett argued the connection between adult education and "useful knowledge" originated in the eighteenth century and continued in the nineteenth century with the development of education institutions like literary clubs, mutual improvement societies, and the lyceum. Under the influence of progressive education and the rise of what Kett called "efficiency educators," adult education became increasingly associated with preparation for work and "job improvement." During the period 1870–1930, technical institutes experienced growth and higher education distanced itself from job training (228–31). According to Kett, in the twentieth century adult education became more formal and tied to institutions of higher learning. Despite its connection to universities through extension and correspondence programs, adult education maintained its focus on practical knowledge aimed at increasing academic and job credentials rather than intellectual development. Adult education's connection to useful and practical knowledge and job improvement has contributed to it being overlooked in discussions of intellectualism.

chapter one
Calls of Crisis and Decline in U.S. Literacy and Learning: Understanding Popular Notions of Intellectualism

1. This hierarchy of knowledge (intellectual vs. useful or practical) is grounded in the historical development of distinct information and cultural markets separated by social class. Historian Richard D. Brown has noted that the information abundance in the mid-nineteenth century amplified by printing presses led to the formation of two distinct information markets. The first, the traditional information market that focused on information for the sake of knowledge, remained under the control of the social elite. The elite maintained control by writing the texts that dominated American education and by dictating the standards of "respectable knowledge." The second, a new information market that formed mid-century, focused on information for entertainment. It was controlled by "popular" audiences and included publications like the penny press (270–77).

2. Simon and Schuster released a 25th Anniversary edition of *Closing* in 2012. In the afterword, journalist Andrew Ferguson argues that "most of Bloom's criticisms still apply. . . . The university we face today is still the one he described, only more so" (391). In 2013, a conference was held to celebrate the twenty-fifth anniversary of the book.
3. E. D. Hirsch Jr. defined "cultural literacy" as the "information that we have traditionally expected our children to receive in school, but which they no longer do" (19). He published a list of what knowledge constitutes cultural literacy in *Cultural Literacy*, and then published a dictionary defining the terms (*The Dictionary of Cultural Literacy: What Every American Needs to Know*) in 1988. He published a revised edition (entitled *The New Dictionary of Cultural Literacy*) in 2002.
4. William Pannapacker published his article under the pseudonym Thomas H. Benton.
5. In his afterword in the 25th Anniversary edition of *The Closing of the American Mind*, Andrew Ferguson called *Academically Adrift* "the most devastating book about higher education since *Closing*" (392–93).
6. The CLA exam is designed to measure critical thinking, analytic reasoning, problem solving, and written communication (20–21). The portion of the CLA exam Arum and Roska focused on in their analysis was the "performance task" that gave students a hypothetical scenario and several related documents and asked them to write a memo (or other form of written response) in which they had to present their evaluation, assessment, and/or recommendation based on the data they were provided (21–22).
7. In *The Last Intellectuals: American Culture in the Age of Academe* (1987), Jacoby argued that beginning in the 1960s, young intellectuals who wrote for the public retreated to the security of university campuses for economic reasons and, as academics, stopped writing for the public.
8. *College English*, *College Composition and Communication*, *Kairos*, *Computers and Composition*, *Composition Forum*, *Composition Studies*, *Journal of Advanced Composition*, *Rhetoric Review*, and *Writing Program Administration*.

chapter two

Intellectualism and the Diffusion of Useful Knowledge: The Nineteenth-Century American Lyceum

1. The word *lyceum* has been used to mean "an institution through which lectures, dramatic performances, debates, and the like are presented to a community," "the association which sponsors such an institution," and "the building in which such lectures, etc., are given" (Bode x–xi). The term originated much earlier and referred to the building or grove near the temple of Apollo Lyceus where Aristotle taught (Hayes viii). In this chapter, I use the word *lyceum* to refer to

nineteenth-century adult education organizations that called themselves lyceums and participated in the lyceum movement begun by Dr. Josiah Holbrook. These organizations included both the lyceum public lecture circuit and local lyceums that held meetings and engaged in discussions and debates. Though town meetings and public lectures were not new activities at the time, lyceum organizations were distinctive in that they were started with the same general plan (designed by Holbrook) and spread significantly.

2. Josiah Holbrook was a teacher and lecturer who studied science at Yale and dedicated himself to popularizing and making accessible to nonspecialists scientific knowledge and technical procedure. He began his career as a keeper of a private school that combined study and farm labor. Before starting the lyceum, he was an itinerant lecturer on scientific subjects. In an effort to realize his goal of spreading knowledge, he not only started the first lyceum in 1826, he also manufactured scientific apparatus for common schools, started two lyceum journals, and in 1837 worked with others to establish a lyceum village in Berea, Ohio.
3. Historian Richard D. Brown ties the increase of these types of societies to a change in the perception of citizenship after the American Revolution: "The new American citizenship idealized political participation and initiative. Public institutions promised responsiveness, flexibility, and improvement as incentives to citizen involvement, while republican ideology warned against apathy as the path toward tyranny" ("The Emergence" 68). Historian Joseph Kett has called the three decades before the Civil War a period "marked by the democratization of knowledge." He calls it primarily a local movement and effort, supported by the transportation revolution, Jacksonian democracy, the lower cost of printed material, the upheaval of the Revolution, and the desire for personal advancement (38–39).
4. Holbrook modeled the lyceum after British and American mechanics' institutes that used a lecture-demonstration method and the creation of local libraries of technical books to teach geometry, mechanics, astronomy, hydrostatics, and chemistry to skilled workingmen.
5. According to communication studies professor John Tapia, the lyceum never flourished in the South because "Southern financial leaders were antagonistic to anything that might upset the slave-based economy, and that included educating blacks and poor whites through lyceum" (13). Carl Bode explained it similarly: "The fundamental fact about the lyceum in the South is that it ran counter to the massive economic and social trends—in which slavery became central—of the region, and to their cultural accompaniment" (Bode 75). He also cites fewer towns, smaller population, and less transportation as reasons for the lyceum's relative absence in the South (76–79).
6. Though the word *lyceum* is never mentioned in this document, the lyceum Holbrook started in the same year is the outcome of his plan for "associations for mutual education" described here.

7. These subjects come from the annals and minutes of the Williams Lyceum Society of Greenfield Academy (1844–46), the Allen Missionary Lyceum of the Ohio Wesleyan University (1846), the Martinsburg Lyceum of Ohio (1842–45), and the South Charleston Lyceum, Ohio (1867–71).
8. *Scientific Tracts* was produced by Josiah Holbrook and others and published by Carter, Hendee, and Babcock. Each issue, about twenty to twenty-five pages in length, educated its readers about a scientific concept or subject. The periodical was published every two weeks for three years under its original name. In 1834, it became *Scientific Tracts and Family Lyceum*.
9. *Family Lyceum* was started by Josiah Holbrook in 1832. It was published in Boston by G. W. Light & Co. Its subtitle demonstrated the commitment to instructing and entertaining the public: "Designed for Instruction and Entertainment, and adapted to Families, Schools, and Lyceums."
10. *Youth's Lyceum*, published monthly by the Columbiana County Lyceum Association in 1837, covered a variety of issues including the earth, the lyceum, sugar, the lever, natural philosophy, gardening, aphorisms, astronomy, history, electricity, and education. It also contained some short stories and poems and juvenile writings. The original text comes from correspondents for the periodical and student prose, while excerpts from periodicals such as *Youth's Magazine* and *American Annals of Education* are also included. The publication cost fifty cents a year in advance and was intended to be readable to a wide, general audience. I had access to vol. 1, no. 1, and vol. 1, no. 6 (1837).
11. As Harvey J. Graff notes in *The Literacy Myth*, access to books and libraries does not mean people read or understood what they read (270–71).
12. The Boston Lyceum Bureau was the first lyceum bureau started by James Redpath.
13. Some of the prominent female lyceum lecturers were Elizabeth Cady Stanton, Susan B. Anthony, Anna Howard Shaw, Julia Ward Howe, Anna Dickinson, and Mary Livermore.
14. Advertisement brochure for the lectures of Dr. Georgia Merriman, titled "Dr. Georgia Merriman Gives Food for Thought in Lectures on Food Analysis." Published by Central Lyceum Bureau. No date on advertisement, but the testimonials are dated 1897.
15. Viola Doudna Romans was a lyceum bureau speaker for the Mutual Lyceum Bureau and for the Central Lyceum Bureau. An Ohio native, she was born in 1863, attended Olney and Muskingham Colleges, and taught elocution and physical culture at Muskingham College and Wesleyan College for Women. She was also involved in the temperance and women's movements and held public offices, including serving as an Ohio House Representative. She was the first woman to represent Franklin County in the Ohio General Assembly. The fliers are not dated. However, they contain quotes from reviews printed in 1902 and 1904.

16. Some of the most famous lecturers at this time were Wendell Phillips, William Lloyd Garrison, Charles Sumner, Henry Ward Beecher, Elizabeth Cady Stanton, Susan B. Anthony, and Julia Ward Howe.
17. Elizabeth Cady Stanton joined James Redpath's Lyceum Bureau in 1859 (Hogan and Hogan 415).
18. According to Carl Bode, Holbrook's leaflet had been printed earlier and went through several editions. However, he said the 1829 version was the most widely circulated and "most influential form of the catalogue of advantages and aims" (23). It was written by Josiah Holbrook, with contributions by Theophilus Rogers Marvin.
19. The Chautauqua movement arose in the mid-1870s and, like the lyceum, offered a traveling circuit of education and entertainment for a low cost; however, it maintained a religious element and tried to disassociate from the lyceum because it felt the lyceum was too commercial and secular and revolved around spectacle and showmanship. The Chautauqua began as a religious camp meeting with religious speakers held every summer at Chautauqua Lake, New York, and developed into small groups of people all over the country (mostly in small towns) reading and discussing books and studying history, music, natural sciences, and classical and modern languages. It prospered, becoming a full-fledged summer school and eventually an organized traveling circuit (Noffsinger 107–11). The Chautauqua circuit eventually became dependent upon bureaus, like the lyceum circuit had. By 1920 the battle between the lyceum circuit and the Chautauqua circuit had nearly disappeared—each one took its place, separate from the other: the Chautauqua was known for its aesthetic quality and drew the suburban-like middle class, while the lyceum drew the middlebrow culture (Rieser 103–4). Eventually, both suffered from the influx of modern entertainment media.
20. Not only did Holbrook envision the lyceum as an educational institution open to all but he also wanted it to be far-reaching. Holbrook's 1826 and 1829 documents reveal Holbrook's full vision of the lyceum as a national movement and force—one that begins with local associations, but includes county, state, and national organizations.

chapter three
Intellectualism and Education for a Practical Purpose: The Twentieth-Century Labor College

1. Joseph Kett wrote, more specifically,

> Under the leadership of Samuel Gompers, the American Federation of Labor evinced little interest in workers' education before 1900. . . . Gompers' well-publicized hostility to intellectuals in the union movement rested on his belief that socialism, anarchism, and other ideologies threatened to subordinate trade unionism to abstract and doomed causes. . . . He endorsed workers' education only to ensure a directing role for the AFL. (352)

Richard J. Altenbaugh also wrote about the failure of the AFL to address workers' issues:

> Put briefly, the policies and actions of the AFL failed to relieve, and in some cases may have intensified, the social and economic plight of American workers by supporting the existing economic system, by aligning itself with a business group whose outlook was anathema to working-class interests, and by ignoring the plight of the majority of workers. ("The Children" 397)

2. Phillips Thompson argued in *The Politics of Labor* that the educational system was biased against workingmen and their families, saying, "Education, for instance, while immensely increasing the power of the working-class for effective combination, if perverted by the inculcation of the untruths and half-truths of bourgeois political economy, is a hindrance rather than a help" (17). For a related discussion of nineteenth-century education and its effect on workers in Canada, see Harvey J. Graff's *The Literacy Myth*, chapter 5.
3. Eugene V. Debs was a union leader, a founding member of the International Labor Union and the Industrial Workers of the World, and was the Socialist Party presidential nominee five times.
4. According to Richard J. Altenbaugh, around ten thousand or so workers were involved in workers' education by the 1920s (*Education* 25). Jonathan Bloom has said that "During the 1920s, a nationwide workers' education movement flourished in the United States. In nearly every U.S. city, some form of labor college or 'workers' university' sprang up after WWI" (71).
5. Richard Dwyer, in "Workers' Education, Labor Education, Labor Studies: An Historical Delineation," argued there were three distinctive historical periods of workers' education in the United States, reflected by changes in curriculum, student body, financial support, general objectives, duration, and administration. He labeled the period from 1900 to 1935 *workers' education* with a focus on social change and a social science curriculum. The students were recruited as individuals and trade unionists. During this period, institutions had independence from the AFL, were long-term schools and programs, and were supported predominantly by liberal sympathizers. He labeled the period from 1935 to 1965 *labor education*, saying it focused on "tool" courses for the purpose of labor organization. The student body during this period was trade unionists who attended short-term courses and conferences. Institutions received trade-union funds or government support and were tied to CIO unions or universities. Dwyer named the period from the 1960s on *labor studies*, claiming education was liberal arts based in the social sciences designed to educate the "whole" man. The programs were either extension programs or rather long-degree programs supported by state governments.
6. Business professor and labor movement leader B. J. Widick criticized union-sponsored programs for being "almost exclusively trade schools" in *Labor Today*,

published by Houghton-Mifflin in 1964. John McCollum, in "Labor Education: Education, Training, or Information?," claimed union-sponsored programs had "very little education and a sizable chunk of training and information" (42). McCollum was director of the Union Research and Education Project at the University of Chicago in 1960.

7. For example, the University of Wisconsin School for Women Workers (started in 1923) trained workers to negotiate and work with employers rather than to be labor activists working for "radical social change" (Altenbaugh, *Education* 53–54).
8. Other examples of university-sponsored workers' education programs include the Bryn Mawr Summer School for Women Workers in Industry and an extension service offered by the University of California. Both programs were started in 1921 and were followed shortly by similar extension programs at Syracuse, Harvard, MIT, Tufts, Amherst, University of Cincinnati, and University of Oklahoma (Altenbaugh, *Education* 46–47).
9. Among the graduates of Brookwood Labor College were Walter Reuther, an organizer of the United Auto Workers; Joseph Ozanic, president of the Progressive Mine Workers of America; and Len De Caux, publicity director of the AFL-CIO (Kates 76; Altenbaugh, *Education* 249–68).
10. According to Joseph Kett, although Brookwood Labor College administrators cooperated with labor groups and local colleges and schools in designing and executing its program, the institution was unaffiliated with a particular union, college, or university (360) and thus had independent reign on the design and implementation of its program. Brookwood's funding came mostly from independent contributions and union scholarship. In 1928, Brookwood received over twelve thousand dollars in contributions and thirty-seven thousand dollars in pledges by unions (Altenbaugh, "The Children" 405). It also received fifty thousand dollars from the American Fund for Public Service (twenty-five thousand dollars in 1927 and the rest over time) to help meet growing expenses (Howlett 55).
11. The archival documents I examined came from the Archives of Labor and Urban Affairs at Wayne State University's Walter P. Reuther Library in Detroit, Michigan, and the Tamiment Library Labor Archives at New York University (NYU).
12. In 1921 the Workers' Education Bureau (WEB) and the Bryn Mawr Summer School for Women Workers in Industry in Pennsylvania were also formed.
13. Sarah Cleghorn was unique among faculty for finding students' "single-minded" purpose troubling. This is not surprising, however, because she was merely kept on as a teacher when Brookwood, having been a preparatory school originally, became a labor college in 1921. She left the school after a short time (Altenbaugh, *Education* 148–49).
14. Many of the autobiographical essays I accessed through the Archives of Labor and Urban Affairs at Wayne State University did not have dates recorded on them. Some of them did not have names. I note any names and dates recorded

on these documents. If I do not mention the date a document was written, it is unknown.

15. For example, according to Altenbaugh, in 1925 a formalized board of directors was formed and students held two of the nineteen positions on the board (*Education* 158).
16. Started in the late nineteenth century, the progressive education movement emphasized experiential and dialogic education. William Mann Fincke was one of the primary founders of Brookwood Labor College. He and his wife Helen intended to create a progressive labor college that would put into practice the ideas of Dewey and other progressive reformers (Kates 80; Altenbaugh, *Education* 70). For a detailed look at the role of progressivism in American education during this period, see Lawrence A. Cremin's *The Transformation of the School: Progressivism in American Education, 1876–1957.*
17. According to the 1924 *Report to the Second International Conference on Workers' Education,* Brookwood's library "contains several thousand volumes and is a very good working library in the social sciences" (1).
18. Director of Brookwood, A. J. Muste wrote about how students were often separated into "research communities" that paired them based on their experience and strengths in terms of reading, researching, organizing, and public speaking (cited in Altenbaugh, "The Children" 404).
19. The teachers whose teaching practices Kates examined included public speaking instructor Josephine Colby, labor journalism instructor Helen Norton, and fieldwork instructor Louis Budenz.
20. Other student publications included the *Brookwood Scroll,* the *Brookwood Wildcat,* and *The Line.* The *Brookwood Scroll* (published by students of the 1936 summer session) contained news flashes from the students' labor organizations, Brookwood sports reports, and a list of the students. *The Line,* subtitled "Student News at Brookwood," was a one-page student publication containing poetry, general announcements, and student gossip in a section titled "Dirt." The tone was sarcastic and humorous. Faculty at Brookwood published (at least once) a page titled *The Firing Line,* a faculty version of *The Line* with the same humor and sarcasm. The *Brookwood Wildcat* was also published by students, weekly, and was described this way: "This paper will be noted for its incompetence, carefree punctuation, and its admirable articulation."
21. Student occupations varied, but included agricultural and industrial workers, cap makers, cab drivers, hosiery knitters, railway carmen, sailors, cooks, migrant workers, and farmers (Altenbaugh, "The Children" 402).
22. Lack of education was largely due to dependence on working at a young age. A little over one-fifth of the students went to work before they were fourteen years old, 38 percent went between ages fourteen and sixteen, and 31 percent went between sixteen and eighteen (*A Census*).

23. While early twentieth-century labor colleges like Brookwood closed their doors mid-century, other forms of workers' education remained. In addition, some of the work of labor colleges has been taken up by various education programs over the years. For example, for many years National Labor College provided workers' education courses and programs for those interested in being union leaders, members, and participants. Other colleges continue to offer workforce education and development programs or specific skills-based career training.
24. National Labor College was the only U.S. regionally accredited higher education institution committed solely to educating union leaders, members, and participants.

chapter four
Intellectualism and Basic Literacy Education: Twenty-First-Century GED Writing Workshops

1. The Lindberg Center is a pseudonym. To maintain confidentiality for all participants in this research, I have changed the names of the educational institution, the students, the teachers, and the program supervisor.
2. My work with the Lindberg Center did not originate with this research. As an outreach consultant for the partnering university, for two years I was one of the graduate students teaching the writing workshops. One year I taught the evening workshops; the other year I taught the day workshops. Though I was no longer teaching at the Lindberg Center when I conducted my research, because I had recently taught at the center, some of the students knew me. This provided a level of comfort and familiarity between the students and me that, I believe, made some of them more willing to be interviewed and more candid during their interviews.
3. Though attendance varied each week in both classes, there were approximately thirty to forty students total (between the two classes) participating in the workshops during the six weeks I observed, surveyed, and interviewed them.
4. While I cannot draw wide definitive conclusions about students' definitions of intellectualism because I only asked six students to define the term, the responses I received from those six students provide some interesting data worth contemplating.
5. Students' distinction between common sense and book smarts is consistent with adult education and literacy scholar Arlene Fingeret's research. Her interviews in the 1980s with "illiterate adults" revealed they associated literate people with a lack of common sense. For these adults, overeducation threatens to change one into what one man calls "a babbling fool" (9).
6. Malcolm was the only student who didn't call himself intelligent. He said "Some people look at me like, Malcolm, you are very intelligent, but I can't see it myself. I can't see it inside me. And I think that's just something holdin' me back."
7. Paul Laurence Dunbar was an African American poet born in 1872 in Dayton, Ohio.

8. The article Matt had students read and discuss was “Obama Debuts Annoying Catchphrase.” It appeared in the “Politics” section of the February 10, 2009, online issue of *The Onion* (Issue 45.07).
9. The paintings were *The Persistence of Memory* by Salvador Dali (1931) and Vincent Van Gogh’s *The Starry Night* (1889).

chapter six
Into the Classroom: Pedagogical Approaches to the Rhetoric of Intellectualism and Anti-intellectualism

1. Unfortunately, I am not able to quote students directly in my description of the class discussion that ensued because I had not anticipated wanting to cite students’ voices in my research and consequently had not applied for IRB approval to ask students for their consent to do so. Instead, I summarize our conversation and students’ contributions to reflect the sentiments they expressed that day.
2. In this section of the chapter, I use students’ real first names because they granted me permission to do so.
3. According to a recent *Academe* article, a survey by the Project on Student Debt concluded that “college seniors who graduated in 2009 carried an average of $24,000 in student-loan debt, up 6 percent from the previous year; at the same time, unemployment among recent college graduates is rising.”

Bibliography

Acceptance letter to Leon A. Cousens, 1934. Box 1, Folder F. Leon Cousens Collection. Archives of Labor and Urban Affairs, Wayne State U, Detroit. Print.

Adler-Kassner, Linda. *The Activist WPA: Changing Stories about Writing and Writers.* Salt Lake City: Utah State UP, 2008. Print.

———. "The Companies We Keep *or* the Companies We Would Like to Try to Keep: Strategies and Tactics in Challenging Times," *WPA* 36.1 (2012): 119–40. Print.

Adler-Kassner, Linda, and Susanmarie Harrington. "Responsibility and Composition's Future in the Twenty-first Century: Reframing 'Accountability.'" CCC 62.1 (2010): 73–99. Print.

Agenda for Student-Faculty Review of the Year's Life and Work at Brookwood. Box 11, Folder 23. Brookwood Labor College Collection. Archives of Labor and Urban Affairs, Wayne State U, Detroit. Print.

Altenbaugh, Richard J. "'The Children and the Instruments of a Militant Labor Progressivism': Brookwood Labor College and the American Labor College Movement of the 1920s and 1930s." *History of Education Quarterly* 23.4 (Winter, 1983): 395–411. Print.

———. *Education for Struggle: The American Labor Colleges of the 1920s and 1930s.* Philadelphia: Temple UP, 1990. Print.

———. "Proletarian Drama: An Educational Tool of the American Labor College Movement." *Theatre Journal* 34.2 (May 1982): 197–210. Print.

Annual Report, 1931–32. Box 6, Folder 9. Brookwood Labor College Collection. Archives of Labor and Urban Affairs, Wayne State U, Detroit. Print.

Annual Report, 1933–34. Box 6, Folder 10. Brookwood Labor College Collection. Archives of Labor and Urban Affairs, Wayne State U, Detroit. Print.

Antczak, Frederick J. *Thought and Character: The Rhetoric of Democratic Education.* Ames: Iowa State UP, 1985. Print.

Arum, Richard. Interviewed by NPR Staff. *Morning Edition.* NPR. 9 Feb. 2011. Web. 15 Feb. 2012.

Arum, Richard, and Josipa Roska. *Academically Adrift: Limited Learning on College Campuses.* Chicago: U of Chicago P, 2011. Print.

———. *Aspiring Adults Adrift: Tentative Transitions of College Graduates.* Chicago: U of Chicago P, 2014. Print.

Bartholomae, David, and Anthony Petrosky. *Facts, Artifacts and Counterfacts: Theory and Method for a Reading and Writing Course.* Upper Montclair, NJ: Boynton /Cook, 1986. Print.

Bauerlein, Mark. *The Dumbest Generation: How the Digital Age Stupifies Young Americans and Jeopardizes Our Future (Or, Don't Trust Anyone under 30)*. New York: Jeremy P. Tarcher/Penguin, 2008. Print.

"Be Stupid" ads. *Diesel.com*. Diesel. Web. 4 Apr. 2011. http://www.diesel.com/be-stupid/.

Behm, Nicholas, Sherry Rankins-Robertson, and Duane Roen. "The Case for Academics as Public Intellectuals." *Academe* (Jan.–Feb. 2014). Web. 6 Mar. 2014.

Benton, Thomas H. "On Stupidity." *Chronicle of Higher Education* 1 Aug. 2008. n. pag. Web. 15 Sept. 2008.

Berlin, James A. *Rhetorics, Poetics, and Cultures: Refiguring College English Studies*. Urbana, IL: NCTE, 1996. Print.

Bilia, Angela, Christopher Dean, Judith Hebb, Monica F. Jacobe, and Doug Sweet. "Forum on Identity." *College English* 73.4 (2011): 379–95. Print.

Bleyer, Willard Grosvenor. Preface. *Newpaper Writing and Editing*. By Bleyer. Boston: Houghton Mifflin, 1913. v–ix. Web. *American Libraries Internet Archive*. 10 Aug. 2012.

Bloom, Allan. *The Closing of the American Mind: How Higher Education Failed Democracy and Impoverished the Souls of Today's Students*. New York: Simon and Schuster, 1987. Print.

Bloom, Jonathan D. "Brookwood Labor College." *The Re-Education of the American Working Class*. Eds. Steven H. London, Elvira R. Tarr, and Joseph F. Wilson. Westport, CT: Greenwood Press, 1990. Print.

Bode, Carl. *The American Lyceum: Town Meeting of the Mind*. New York: Oxford UP, 1956. Print.

"Books Used in Courses at Brookwood Labor College." Box 11, Folder 23. Brookwood Collection. Archives of Labor and Urban Affairs, Wayne State U, Detroit. Print.

Bousquet, Mark. *How the University Works: Higher Education and the Low-Wage Nation*. New York: NYU Press, 2008. Print.

Branch, Kirk. "From the Margins at the Center: Literacy, Authority, and the Great Divide." CCC 50.2 (1998): 206–31. Print.

Brigance, William Norwood, ed. *A History and Criticism of American Public Address*. Vol. 1. New York: McGraw-Hill, 1943. Print.

Brookwood Bulletin and Announcement of Labor Courses, 1931–32. Box 2, Folder 22. Katherine Pollak Ellickson Collection. Archives of Labor and Urban Affairs, Wayne State U, Detroit. Print.

Brookwood Fellowship Review 1.1 (November 1926). Box 93, Folder 3. Brookwood Labor College Collection. Archives of Labor and Urban Affairs, Wayne State U, Detroit. Print.

Brookwood Labor College. 1925. Box 25, Folder 8. Mark and Helen Norton Starr Collection. Archives of Labor and Urban Affairs, Wayne State U, Detroit. Print.

The Brookwood Labor Pamphlets. Box 11, Folder 22. Brookwood Labor College Collection. Archives of Labor and Urban Affairs, Wayne State U, Detroit. Print.

Brookwood Labor Players. Box 98, Folder 5. Brookwood Labor College Collection. Archives of Labor and Urban Affairs, Wayne State U, Detroit. Print.

Brookwood Review 1.4 (15 Apr. 1923). Box 7, Folder 13. The Mark and Helen Norton Starr Collection. Archives of Labor and Urban Affairs, Wayne State U, Detroit. Print.

Brookwood Review 2.1 (1 Dec. 1923). Box 7, Folder 13. Mark and Helen Norton Starr Collection. Archives of Labor and Urban Affairs, Wayne State U, Detroit. Print.

Brookwood Review 2.2 (1 Jan. 1924). Box 7, Folder 13. Mark and Helen Norton Starr Collection. Archives of Labor and Urban Affairs, Wayne State U, Detroit. Print.

Brookwood Review 10.2 (Feb. 1932). Katherine Pollak Ellickson Collection. Archives of Labor and Urban Affairs, Wayne State U, Detroit. Print.

Brookwood Wildcat. Box 96, Folder 9. Brookwood Labor College Collection. Archives of Labor and Urban Affairs, Wayne State U, Detroit. Print.

Brookwood's Contribution to the Labor Movement: Fourteen Years of Service. Box 25, Folder 8. Mark and Helen Norton Starr Collection. Archives of Labor and Urban Affairs, Wayne State U, Detroit. Print.

Brown, Richard D. "The Emergence of Voluntary Associations in Massachusetts, 1760–1830." *Journal of Voluntary Action Research* 2.2 (1973): 64–73. Print.

——. *Knowledge Is Power: The Diffusion of Information in Early America, 1700–1865.* New York: Oxford UP, 1989. Print.

Carlson, Kenneth D. "Labor Education in America." *Review of Educational Research* 41.2 (1971): 115–30. Print.

Carr, Nicholas. *The Glass Cage: Automation and Us.* New York: W. W. Norton, 2014. Print.

——. "Is Google Making Us Stupid?" *The Atlantic* (July/Aug. 2008). n. pag. Web. 15 Sept. 2008.

——. *The Shallows: What the Internet Is Doing to Our Brains.* New York: W. W. Norton, 2010. Print.

Cascio, Jamais. "Get Smart." *The Atlantic* (July/Aug. 2009): 94–100. Print.

A Census of Brookwood Students: A Study Made by a Class in Statistics at Brookwood Labor College, 1927. Box 1, Folder 1. Brookwood Labor College Collection. Archives of Labor and Urban Affairs, Wayne State U, Detroit. Print.

Clark, Carroll D. "Non-Academic Higher Education." *Journal of Higher Education* 3.8 (1932): 401–6. Print.

Claussen, Dane S. "A Brief History of Anti-intellectualism in American Media." *Academe* 97.3 (2011): 8–13. *ERIC.* 16 Aug. 2011.

Cohn, Fannia M. "Brookwood's Strength: Relating Facts to Ideas." *Fifteenth Anniversary Review.* 9–10; 89. Box 13, Folder 10. Brookwood Labor College Collection. Archives of Labor and Urban Affairs, Wayne State U, Detroit. Print.

Colby, Josephine. Course materials. Box 3, Folder 20. Brookwood Labor College Collection. Archives of Labor and Urban Affairs, Wayne State U, Detroit. Print.

Columbiana County Lyceum Association. *Youth's Lyceum* 1.1–6 (1837). Ohio Historical Society Archives, Columbus. Print.

Common Core State Standards. Common Core State Standards Initiative. Web. 30 Jan. 2015. http://www.corestandards.org/.

Correspondence Courses for Workers. Box 25, Folder 8. Mark and Helen Norton Starr Collection. Archives of Labor and Urban Affairs, Wayne State U, Detroit. Print.

Curriculum Report, 1925–26. Box 6, Folder 6. Brookwood Labor College Collection. Archives of Labor and Urban Affairs, Wayne State U, Detroit. Print.

Curtis, Henry Barnes. "Inaugural Address of the President of the Mount Vernon Lyceum, 1834." PA Box 34, 16. Ohio Historical Society Archives, Columbus. Print.

Deresiewicz, William. *Excellent Sheep: The Miseducation of the American Elite and the Way to a Meaningful Life*. New York: Free Press, 2014. Print.

de Zengotita, Thomas. "The Numbing of the American Mind: Culture as Anesthetic." *Harper's* (Apr. 2002): 33–40. Print.

Dickson, Marcia. *It's Not Like That Here: Teaching Academic Writing and Reading to Novice Writers*. Portsmouth, NH: Heinemann-Boynton/Cook, 1995. Print.

Digital Nation: Life on the Virtual Frontier. Frontline. PBS. 2010. Film.

Donoghue, Frank. *The Last Professors: The Corporate University and the Fate of the Humanities*. New York: Fordham UP, 2008. Print.

Dornbusch, Sophie R. Autobiography. Box 93, Folder 2. Brookwood Labor College Collection. Archives of Labor and Urban Affairs, Wayne State U, Detroit. Print.

Dwyer, Richard. "Workers' Education, Labor Education, Labor Studies: An Historical Delineation." *Review of Educational Research* 47.1 (1977): 179–207. Print.

Ede, Lisa. *Situating Composition: Composition Studies and the Politics of Location*. Carbondale: Southern Illinois UP, 2004. Print.

Edmundson, Mark. "On the Uses of a Liberal Education: I. As Lite Entertainment for Bored College Students." *Harper's* (Sept. 1997): 39–49. Print.

———. *Why Teach? In Defense of a Real Education*. New York: Bloomsbury, 2013. Print.

Eldred, Janet Carey, and Peter Mortensen. "Reading Literacy Narratives." *College English* 54.5 (1992): 512–39. Print.

English, Elizabeth. Course materials. Box 1, Folder 18. Roy Reuther Collection. Archives of Labor and Urban Affairs, Wayne State U, Detroit. Print.

Farquhar, William Henry. *Annals of Sandy Spring of Twenty Years History of a Rural Community in Maryland*. Vol. 1. Baltimore: Cushing and Bailey, 1884. Ohio Historical Society Archives. Columbus. Print.

Fehnel, Paul W. Autobiography. Box 93, Folder 2. Brookwood Labor College Collection. Archives of Labor and Urban Affairs, Wayne State U, Detroit. Print.

Fifteenth Anniversary Review. Box 13, Folder 10. Brookwood Labor College Collection. Archives of Labor and Urban Affairs, Wayne State U, Detroit. Print.

Fingeret, Arlene. “Through the Looking Glass: Literacy as Perceived by Illiterate Adults.” Annual meeting of the American Educational Research Association, New York, Mar. 1982. Print.

Freire, Paulo, and Donald Macedo. *Literacy: Reading the Word and the World*. South Hadley, MA: Bergin and Garvey P, 1984. Print.

Gee, James Paul. *The Anti-Education Era: Creating Smarter Students through Digital Learning*. New York: Palgrave Macmillan, 2013. Print.

Giroux, Henry A. “The Disappearing Intellectual in the Age of Economic Darwinism.” *Truthout* (13 July 2010). Web. 13 Jan. 2015.

———. *The Mouse That Roared: Disney and the End of Innocence*. Lanham, MD: Rowman and Littlefield, 1999. Print.

———. “Noam Chomsky and the Public Intellectual in Turbulent Times.” *Truthout* (12 May 2014). Web. 13 Jan. 2015.

Giroux, Susan Searls. “The Age of Unreason: Race and the Drama of American Anti-Intellectualism.” *JAC* 29.1–2 (2009): 295–352. Print.

Gitlin, Todd. “The Renaissance of Anti-Intellectualism.” *Chronicle Review* (8 Dec. 2000): B7–B9. Print.

Goodhue, Everett W. Rev. of *Principles of the New Economics*, by Lionel Danforth Edie. *American Economic Review* 12.4 (1922): 624–25. *JSTOR*. Web. 10 Aug. 2012.

Graff, Harvey J. *The Literacy Myth: Cultural Integration and Social Structure in the Nineteenth Century*. New Brunswick, NJ: Transaction, 1991. Print.

———. “The Literacy Myth at Thirty.” *Journal of Social History* (Spring 2010). 635–61. Print.

Gramsci, Antonio. *Selections from the Prison Notebooks*. Trans. Quentin Hoare and Geoffrey Nowell Smith. New York: International Publishers, 1971. Print.

Grattan, C. Hartley. *In Quest of Knowledge: A Historical Perspective on Adult Education*. New York: Association Press, 1955. Print.

Gray-Rosendale, Laura. *Rethinking Basic Writing: Exploring Identity, Politics, and Community in Interaction*. Mahwah, NJ: Lawrence Erlbaum Associates, 2000. Print.

Greene, Nicole Pepinster, and Patricia J. McAlexander, eds. *Basic Writing in America: The History of Nine College Programs*. Cresskill, NJ: Hampton Press, 2008. Print.

Harris, Joseph. *A Teaching Subject: Composition since 1966*. Upper Saddle River, NJ: Prentice-Hall, 1997. Print.

Hayes, Cecil B. *The American Lyceum: Its History and Contribution to Education*. Bulletin No. 12. Washington, DC: US Department of the Interior Office of Education, 1932. Print.

Hayes, Dianne Williams. “Athletes, Outcasts, and Partyers.” *Black Issues in Higher Education* 12.23 (1996): 26–28. Print.

Hirsch, Jr., E. D. *Cultural Literacy: What Every American Needs to Know*. Boston: Houghton Mifflin, 1987. Print.

Hobson, J. A. Rev. of *Industrial Society*. *Economic Journal* 40.160 (1930): 667–69. *JSTOR*. Web. 10 Aug. 2012.

Hofstadter, Richard. *Anti-intellectualism in American Life*. New York: Knopf, 1963. Print.

———. "Democracy and Anti-intellectualism in America." *Michigan Alumnus Quarterly Review* 59 (1953): 281–95. Print.

Hogan, Lisa S., and Michael Hogan. "Feminine Virtue and Practical Wisdom: Elizabeth Cady Stanton's 'Our Boys.'" *Rhetoric & Public Affairs* 6.3 (2003): 415–36. Print.

Holbrook, Josiah. *American Lyceum, or Society for the Improvement of Schools and Diffusion of Useful Knowledge*. Boston: Perkins and Marvin, 1829. *Google Book Search*. Web. 12 July 2007.

———. "Associations of Adults for Mutual Education." *American Journal of Education* (Oct. 1826): 594–97. *Google Book Search*. Web. 10 July 2007.

Holbrook, Josiah and others. *The Family Lyceum* 1.1 (July 1832): 1. Ohio Historical Society Archives, Columbus. Print.

———. *Scientific Tracts, Designed for Instruction and Entertainment, and Adapted to Schools, Lyceums and Families*. Vol. 1. Boston: Carter, Hendee, and Babcock, 1831. American Libraries Internet Archive. Web. 14 Aug. 2007.

———. *Scientific Tracts, Designed for Instruction and Entertainment, and Adapted to Schools, Lyceums and Families*. Vol. 8. Boston: Carter, Hendee, and Babcock, 1831. American Libraries Internet Archive. Web. 14 Aug. 2007.

Horner, Charles F. *The Life of James Redpath and the Development of the Modern Lyceum*. New York: Barse and Hopkins, 1926. Print.

Howlett, Charles F. *Brookwood Labor College and the Struggle for Peace and Social Justice in America*. Lewiston, NY: Edwin Mellen Press, 1993. Print.

Hyman, Colette. *Staging Strikes: Workers' Theatre and the American Labor Movement*. Philadelphia: Temple UP, 1997. Print.

Jacoby, Russell. *The Last Intellectuals: American Culture in the Age of Academe*. New York: Basic Books, 1987. Print.

Jacoby, Susan. *The Age of American Unreason*. New York: Pantheon Books, 2008. Print.

Johnson, Nan. *Gender and Rhetorical Space in American Life, 1866–1910*. Carbondale: Southern Illinois UP, 2002. Print.

Johnson, Steven. *Everything Bad Is Good for You: How Today's Popular Culture Is Actually Making Us Smarter*. New York: Riverhead Books, 2006. Print.

———. "Watching TV Makes You Smarter." *New York Times Magazine* (24 Apr. 2005): 54–59. *InfoTrac Custom Newspapers*. Web. 9 Feb. 2010.

Kates, Susan. *Activist Rhetorics and American Higher Education, 1885–1937*. Carbondale: Southern Illinois UP, 2001. Print.

———. "Emerging Technologies and the Public Intellectual." *Literature Interpretation Theory* 16 (2005): 381–88. Print.

Keeling, Richard, and Richard Hersh. *We're Losing Our Minds: Rethinking American Higher Education*. New York: Palgrave Macmillan, 2011. Print.

Keister, Albert S. Rev. of *Industrial Society*, by Leon Carroll. *Annals of the American Academy of Political and Social Science* 152 (1930): 421. *JSTOR*. Web. 10 Aug. 2012.

Kett, Joseph F. *The Pursuit of Knowledge under Difficulties: From Self-Improvement to Adult Education in America, 1750–1990*. Stanford: Stanford UP, 1994. Print.

Kimball, Roger. *Tenured Radicals: How Politics Has Corrupted Our Higher Education*. Chicago: Elephant Paperbacks, 1998. Print.

Kuhlman, G., and A. Pierce. *Student Memorandum, 1931–32*. Box 96, Folder 6. Brookwood Labor College Collection. Archives of Labor and Urban Affairs, Wayne State U, Detroit. Print.

Lasch, Christopher. *The Culture of Narcissism: American Life in an Age of Diminishing Expectations*. New York: W. W. Norton, 1979. Print.

———. *The Revolt of the Elites and the Betrayal of Democracy*. New York: W. W. Norton, 1995. Print.

Lefkowitz, Abraham. "The Control of Education." *Fifteenth Anniversary Review*. 56–57. Box 13, Folder 10. Brookwood Labor College Collection. Archives of Labor and Urban Affairs, Wayne State U, Detroit. Print.

Levine, Lawrence. *Highbrow/Lowbrow: The Emergence of Cultural Hierarchy in America*. Cambridge: Harvard UP, 1988. Print.

———. *The Opening of the American Mind: Canons, Culture, and History*. Boston: Beacon Press, 1996. Print.

Lim, Elvin T. "Five Trends in Presidential Rhetoric: An Analysis of Rhetoric from George Washington to Bill Clinton." *Presidential Studies Quarterly* 32.2 (2002): 328–66. Print.

Lu, Min-Zhan. "Conflict and Struggle: The Enemies or Preconditions of Basic Writing?" *College English* 54 (1992): 887–913. Print.

Martindale, John S. "Carrying Brookwood to the Workers." *Fifteenth Anniversary Review* 24. Box 13, Folder 10. Brookwood Labor College Collection. Archives of Labor and Urban Affairs, Wayne State U, Detroit. Print.

———. "Workers' Education and Dramatics." *Fifteenth Anniversary Review* 44. Box 13, Folder 10. Brookwood Labor College Collection. Archives of Labor and Urban Affairs, Wayne State U, Detroit. Print.

McCollum, John. "Labor Education: Education, Training, or Information?" *Adult Education Quarterly* 13 (1962): 42–48. Print.

McCormick, Samuel. *Letters to Power: Public Advocacy without Public Intellectualism*. University Park, PA: Penn State UP, 2011. Print.

McLemee, Scott. "Deconstructing Composition: The 'New Theory Wars' Break Out in an Unlikely Discipline." *Chronicle of Higher Education*. Web. 21 Mar. 2003.

Mead, David. *Yankee Eloquence in the Middle West: The Ohio Lyceum 1850–1870.* East Lansing: Michigan State College P, 1951. Print.

Memorandum on Entrance Requirements Brookwood Labor College, 1927. Box 6, Folder 1. Brookwood Labor College Collection. Archives of Labor and Urban Affairs, Wayne State U, Detroit. Print.

Minute Book, 1842–45 for Martinsburg Lyceum of Martinsburg, Ohio. Ohio Historical Society Archives. Columbus. Print.

Minute Book, 1844–46, Williams Lyceum Society of Greenfield Academy. Lancaster, Ohio. Ohio Historical Society Archives. Columbus. Print.

Modern Industry Course Materials. Box 5, Folder 2. Brookwood Labor College Collection. Archives of Labor and Urban Affairs, Wayne State U, Detroit. Print.

Muste, A. J. Letter. 23 Apr. 1929. Box 13, Folder 7. Brookwood Labor College Collection. Archives of Labor and Urban Affairs, Wayne State U, Detroit. Print.

Mutnick, Deborah. *Writing in an Alien World: Basic Writing and the Struggle for Equality in Higher Education.* Portsmouth, NH: Boynton/Cook, 1996. Print.

National Endowment for the Arts. *Reading at Risk: A Survey of Literary Reading in America.* Washington: NEA, 2004. Print.

National Labor College. The National Labor College. Web. 15 July 2014.

Nilsson, Harry. "Grads Come Through." *Fifteenth Anniversary Review* 27–28. Box 13, Folder 10. Brookwood Labor College Collection. Archives of Labor and Urban Affairs, Wayne State U, Detroit. Print.

Noffsinger, John S. *Correspondence Schools, Lyceums, Chautauquas.* New York: MacMillan, 1926. Print.

Nordstrom, George. Autobiography. Box 93, Folder 2. Brookwood Labor College Collection. Archives of Labor and Urban Affairs, Wayne State U, Detroit. Print.

Norton, Helen G. Course materials. Box 4, Folder 11. Brookwood Labor College Collection. Archives of Labor and Urban Affairs, Wayne State U, Detroit. Print.

———. Course materials. Box 4, Folder 12. Brookwood Labor College Collection. Archives of Labor and Urban Affairs, Wayne State U, Detroit. Print.

The Official Be Stupid Philosophy. Diesel.com. Web. 4 Apr. 2011.

Olson, Gary A., ed. *Rhetoric and Composition as Intellectual Work.* Carbondale: Southern Illinois UP, 2002. Print.

Otte, George, and Rebecca Williams Mlynarczyk. *Basic Writing.* West Lafayette, IN: Parlor Press and WAC Clearinghouse, 2010. Print.

Oxford English Dictionary. John Simpson and Edmund Weiner, eds. Oxford: Clarendon Press; New York: Oxford University Press, 1989. Print.

Palmeri, Jason. *Remixing Composition: A History of Multimodal Writing Pedagogy.* NCTE, 2012. Print.

Pearson, Rhoda. Autobiography. Box 93, Folder 2. Brookwood Labor College Collection. Archives of Labor and Urban Affairs, Wayne State U, Detroit. Print.

"Plan Workers' College." *New York Times* 1 Apr. 1921. *New York Times Archives*. Web. 16 Dec. 2007.

Posner, Richard A. *Public Intellectuals: A Study of Decline*. Cambridge: Harvard UP, 2001. Print.

Powell, E. P. "The Rise and Decline of the New England Lyceum." *New England Magazine* 17.6 (Feb. 1895): 730–39. Print.

Press Release, 1932. "New Labor Pamphlet Series Is Simple, Direct." Box 12, Folder 6. Brookwood Labor College Collection. Archives of Labor and Urban Affairs, Wayne State U, Detroit. Print.

Press Release, 1934. Box 12, Folder 15. Brookwood Labor College Collection. Archives of Labor and Urban Affairs, Wayne State U, Detroit. Print.

Promotional Flyer. *Dr. Georgia Merriman, Gives Food for Thought in Lectures on Food Analysis*. PA Box 144, 44. Cleveland: Central Lyceum Bureau. Ohio Historical Society Archives. Columbus. Print.

Promotional Flyer. *Lyceum Entertainers*. "Traveling Culture: Circuit Chautauqua in the Twentieth Century." The Library of Congress American Memory. Web. 14 Aug. 2007.

Promotional Flyer. *Viola Doudna Romans, Lecturer.* Chicago: Mutual Lyceum Bureau. Viola D. Romans Papers, 1803–1945. Ohio Historical Society Archives. Columbus. Print.

Promotional Flyer. *Viola Doudna Romans, Popular Lectures*. Columbus: Central Lyceum Bureau. Viola D. Romans Papers, 1803–1945. Ohio Historical Society Archives. Columbus. Print.

Questionnaire for Prospective Brookwood Students. Box 61, Folder 8. Brookwood Labor College Collection. Archives of Labor and Urban Affairs, Wayne State U, Detroit. Print.

Rankins-Robertson, Sherry, Tiffany Bourelle, and Duane Roen. "Enhancing Learning and Thinking in Higher Education." *WPA* 35.2 (2012): 196–206. Print.

Ravitch, Diane. *The Death and Life of the American School System: How Testing and Choice Are Undermining Education*. New York: Basic Books, 2010. Print.

Ray, Angela G. *The Lyceum and Public Culture in the Nineteenth-Century United States*. East Lansing: Michigan State UP, 2005. Print.

Records, 1846, of the Allen Missionary Lyceum of the Ohio Wesleyan University. Delaware, Ohio. Ohio Historical Society Archives. Columbus. Print.

Records, 1867–71, of the South Charleston Lyceum, Ohio. Ohio Historical Society Archives. Columbus. Print.

Report of Brookwood Executive Committee to Annual Meeting of Board of Directors and of Brookwood, Inc., 1927. Box 6, Folder 6. Brookwood Labor College Collection. Archives of Labor and Urban Affairs, Wayne State U, Detroit. Print.

Report on Lyceum. *Cleveland Herald*. 1841. Ohio Historical Society Archives. Columbus. Print.

Report to the Second International Conference on Workers' Education, 1924. Box 12, Folder 22. Brookwood Labor College Collection. Archives of Labor and Urban Affairs, Wayne State U, Detroit. Print.

Rev. of *Labor Attitudes and Problems*, by W. E. Atkins and H. D. Laswell. *University Journal of Business* 4.2 (1926): 204–5. *JSTOR*. Web. 10 Aug. 2012.

Review of Lyceum. *Cleveland Herald and Gazette*. Oct. 1838. Ohio Historical Society Archives. Columbus. Print.

"Reviews." Of *Academically Adrift*. *CCC* 63.3 (2012): 487–506. Print.

Rieser, Andrew. *The Chautauqua Moment: Protestants, Progressives, and the Culture of Modern Liberalism*. New York: Columbus UP, 2003. Print.

Rose, Mike. *Back to School: Why Everyone Deserves a Second Chance at Education*. New York: The New Press, 2012. Print.

———. "Intelligence, Knowledge, and the Hand/Brain Divide." *Phi Delta Kappan* 89.9 (2008). n. pag. Web. 12 June 2009.

———. Interview by Liane Hansen. *Weekend Edition Sunday*. NPR. 5 Sept. 2004. Web. 5 Jan. 2012.

———. *Lives on the Boundary*. New York: Free Press, 1989. Print.

———. *The Mind at Work: Valuing the Intelligence of the American Worker*. New York: Viking, 2004. Print.

———. "Narrowing the Mind and Page: Remedial Writers and Cognitive Reductionism." *College Composition and Communication* 39.3 (1988): 267–302. Print.

———. *Why School? Reclaiming Education for All of Us*. New York: The New Press, 2009. Print.

Rosenfield, Alvom. Autobiography. Box 93, Folder 1. Brookwood Labor College Collection. Archives of Labor and Urban Affairs, Wayne State U, Detroit. Print.

Scribner, Sylvia, and Michael Cole. *The Psychology of Literacy*. Cambridge: Harvard UP, 1981. Print.

Scott, Donald M. "The Popular Lecture and the Creation of a Public in Mid-Nineteenth-Century America." *Journal of American History* 66.4 (1980): 791–809. Print.

Sedgwick, Theodore. *The Practicability of the Abolition of Slavery: A Lecture, Delivered at the Lyceum in Stockbridge, Massachusetts, February, 1831*. The Cornell University Library Digital Collection. Print.

Selber, Stuart A. "The Social Formation of Technical Communication Studies." CCC 50.2 (1998): 263–76. Print.

Selfe, Cynthia L. *Technology and Literacy in the Twenty-First Century: The Importance of Paying Attention*. Carbondale: Southern Illinois UP, 1999. Print.

Shaughnessy, Mina. *Errors and Expectations: A Guide for the Teacher of Basic Writing*. New York: Oxford UP, 1977. Print.

Sheils, Merrill. "Why Johnny Can't Write." *Newsweek* (8 Dec. 1975): 58–63. Web.

Shor, Ira. *The Culture Wars: School and Society in the Conservative Restoration*. Chicago: U of Chicago P, 1992. Print.

——. *Empowering Education: Critical Teaching for Social Change*. Chicago: U of Chicago P, 1992. Print.

Shorris, Earl. "On the Uses of a Liberal Education: II. As a Weapon in the Hands of the Restless Poor." *Harper's* (Sept. 1997): 50–60. Print.

Skoble, Aeon J. "Lisa and American Anti-Intellectualism." *"The Simpsons" and Philosophy: The D'oh! of Homer*. Ed. William Irwin, Mark Conrad, and Aeon Skoble. Chicago and La Salle: Open Court, 2001. 24–34. Print.

Smith, Tucker P. "Brookwood: No Longer an Experiment." *Fifteenth Anniversary Review*. 7–8; 88. Box 13, Folder 10. Brookwood Labor College Collection. Archives of Labor and Urban Affairs, Wayne State U, Detroit. Print.

Stambler, Leah G. "The Lyceum Movement in American Education, 1826–1845." *Paedagogica Historica* 21 (1981): 157–85. Print.

Stanley, Jane. *The Rhetoric of Remediation: Negotiating Entitlement and Access to Higher Education*. Pittsburgh: U of Pittsburgh P, 2010. Print.

Starr, Mark. Course materials. Box 2, Folder 3. Brookwood Labor College Collection. Archives of Labor and Urban Affairs, Wayne State U, Detroit. Print.

Street, Brian. *Social Literacies: Critical Approaches to Literacy in Development, Ethnography and Education*. New York: Longman, 1995. Print.

Strobel, John. Autobiography. Box 93, Folder 1. Brookwood Labor College Collection. Archives of Labor and Urban Affairs, Wayne State U, Detroit. Print.

Student Petition, 1932. Box 96, Folder 3. Brookwood Labor College Collection. Archives of Labor and Urban Affairs, Wayne State U, Detroit. Print.

Suggested Brief Statement of Purpose. 1929. Box 1, Folder 3. Brookwood Labor College Collection. Archives of Labor and Urban Affairs, Wayne State U, Detroit. Print.

A Survey of Brookwood Students, 1921–1931. Box 96, Folder 11. Brookwood Labor College Collection. Archives of Labor and Urban Affairs, Wayne State U, Detroit. Print.

Svehla, Lance. "Philosopher-Kings and Teacher-Researchers: The Charge of Anti-intellectualism in Composition's Theory Wars." *TETYC* (May 2001): 383–92. Print.

Tapia, John E. *Circuit Chautauqua: From Rural Education to Popular Entertainment in Early Twentieth Century America*. Jefferson, NC: McFarland and Co., 1997. Print.

Thompson, Phillips. *The Politics of Labor*. New York and Chicago: Belford, Clarke, and Co. P, 1887. Print.

Twelfth Anniversary Review. Box 13, Folder 10. Brookwood Labor College Collection. Archives of Labor and Urban Affairs, Wayne State U, Detroit. Print.

Unknown student. Autobiography. Box 93, Folder 1. Brookwood Labor College Collection. Archives of Labor and Urban Affairs, Wayne State U, Detroit. Print.

Unknown student (first name Ben). Autobiography. Box 93, Folder 1. Brookwood Labor College Collection. Archives of Labor and Urban Affairs, Wayne State U, Detroit. Print.

Unnamed woman. Autobiography. Box 93, Folder 1. Brookwood Labor College Collection. Archives of Labor and Urban Affairs, Wayne State U, Detroit. Print.

Upper Alton Lyceum. *Notice at the Next Regular Meeting of the Upper Alton Lyceum*. 1839. Printed Ephemera Collection; Portfolio 15, Folder 15. The Library of Congress American Memory. Web. 12 July 2014.

Villanueva, Victor. *Bootstraps: From an American Academic of Color.* Urbana, IL: NCTE, 1993. Print.

Walker, Timothy. "Address, Delivered at the Opening of the Charlestown Lyceum: January 5, 1830." Miscellaneous Matter; 21. Ohio Historical Society Archives. Columbus. Print.

Watts, V. Orval. Rev. of *American Economic Life*, by Rexford G. Tugwell, Thomas Munro, and Roy E. Stryker, eds. *Economic Geography* 2.3 (1926): 451–52. *JSTOR*. Web. 10 Aug. 2012.

Weisser, Christian. *Moving beyond Academic Discourse: Composition Studies and the Public Sphere*. Carbondale: Southern Illinois UP, 2002. Print.

Weld, W. E. Rev. of *The Worker in Modern Economic Society*, by Paul H. Douglas, Curtice N. Hitchcocks, and Willard E. Atkins. *Political Science Quarterly* 39.3 (1924): 531–32. *JSTOR*. Web. 10 Aug. 2012.

West Medford Library and Lyceum Association. *Lyceum Lecture*. Printed Ephemera Collection; Portfolio 61, Folder 1. The Library of Congress American Memory. Web. 14 Aug. 2014.

Widick, B. J. *Labor Today: The Triumphs and Failures of Unionism in the United States*. Boston: Houghton-Mifflin, 1964. Print.

Workers' Education Bureau of America. *Workers' Education in the United States: Report of Proceedings First National Conference on Workers' Education in the United States*. New York: Workers' Education Bureau, 1921. Web. *GoogleBooks*. 14 Aug. 2014.

Index

KELLY SUSAN BRADBURY TEACHES WRITING and rhetoric at the University of Colorado Boulder. Her work has appeared in *The Best of the Independent Rhetoric and Composition Journals 2012*, *Community Literacy Journal*, *Computers and Composition*, and *Journal of Teaching Writing*.